❝ *This is one of my favorite go-to books for mindfulness and yoga in my 4th grade classroom! I'm a big fan of the child-centered, interactive, accessible, and just plain fun lessons! After our Classroom in Balance work, my students share that they feel more calm, energized, and balanced for the day of learning ahead! I am, too!*

~ Kristen Mimlitz,
4th grade teacher / Chicago, IL

❝ *I use A Classroom in Balance with my 8th grade students at the beginning of each class period to center and prepare them for our time together. Watching my students focus on their thoughts, breathing, and movement is one of the highlights of my time with them and a great use of our time. It's extremely rewarding to observe and hear about my 8th graders practicing these techniques across class settings, even when I'm not there to lead them. It has created an overall positive culture within our classroom. This resource is the best investment I've made for my students and should be in every classroom.*

~ Liz Frazier
8th Grade Special Education & Literacy Teacher / Cedar Rapids, IA

❝ *A Classroom in Balance has provided a multitude of learning opportunities for everyone in the class: students, teachers, and support staff. We all look forward to the time set aside for the range of activities from silent reflection to organized group discussion & movement. This book has allowed social-emotional learning to take a greater role in my weekly plan, while enhancing the students' overall well-being.*

~ Miah Betz
High School History Teacher / Jessup, IA

❝ *For me, using mindfulness every class period puts me in the right headspace to be motivated to learn and keep progressing throughout my day. (With Mindfulness) I feel like I have something to fall back on in times of stress to get me back on track, regain focus, and keep moving forward.*

~ Carleigh Jefford
High School Student taught from A Classroom in Balance / DeWitt, IA

❝ *Starting class with Mindfulness was a really great experience for me. It was a great way to take a break from the chaos of my day. It allowed me to reset and focus on myself and my mental health for a moment.*

~ Ethan Dickey
High School Student taught from A Classroom in Balance / DeWitt, IA

A CLASSROOM IN
BALANCE

Helping Your Students Connect Their Minds, Bodies,
and Hearts through the Practice of Mindfulness

By Julie Strittmatter

challenge
to change

Challenge to Change, Inc.
www.challengetochangeinc.com

Ordering Information:
For details, contact grow@challengetochangeinc.com.

Paperback ISBN: 978-1-7363264-0-4
eBook ISBN:978-1-7363264-1-1

Second Edition

This book is for all who teach and all who learn.

For each person who helps compassionately raise our children in classrooms, on sporting fields, in spirituality centers, and anywhere that learning takes place.

Thank you for honoring the truth that teaching in any capacity is more than offering knowledge; it is sharing wisdom and heart.

Thank you for sharing your wisdom and your heart.

We see you.
We honor you.
We support you.
We thank you.

• FOREWORD •
Molly Schreiber

Yoga and Mindfulness returned to my life at a time when I had left my job teaching in the elementary classroom to raise my three beautiful children and then found myself unexpectedly widowed. Although this was arguably the most challenging time of my life, I believe it was the perfect time for me to deepen my practice as Yoga and Mindfulness taught me how to slow down and connect with myself. I was able to see myself transform from the inside out as my daily commitment to these practices grew in time and depth.

Eventually I made my way back into the role of a classroom teacher, and I quickly noticed how drastically schools had changed in just a few short years. Students seemed more anxious, the school day felt a bit more hurried, and teachers appeared more stressed. It was during this time that I decided children needed the practices or Yoga and Mindfulness, too.

The Dali Lama once said, **"If every 8 year old in the world is taught meditation, we will eliminate violence from the world within one generation."** When I taught my students Yoga and Mindfulness, whether it was for five minutes or an hour, I believed what the Dali Lama said was true, and I felt so much hope for the future. It was this hope that inspired me to start Challenge to Change.

I opened the doors to our yoga studio in Dubuque, Iowa, where we offered children's and family fitness classes, and I began a partnership with the elementary schools in our area to bring Yoga and Mindfulness into the elementary classrooms once a month. Soon, however, I realized this wasn't enough. I wanted to continue to bring these practices to our youth as they entered their middle and high school years.

Instead of hoping on a wish and prayer that the children would continue to practice Yoga on their own in their adolescent years, I decided it was time to expand Challenge to Change's mission to include middle school and high school programming. As an elementary educator and a children's yoga instructor, I knew my expertise was in working with younger children. I needed someone with a shared passion for Yoga and Mindfulness who had experience working with older youth.

Julie Strittmatter was a high school english teacher and an adult yoga instructor who shared my enthusiasm for our vision. She spoke her truth about wanting to create Mindfulness programming to support secondary education students and teachers. Julie was the perfect person to make what was once a one lane journey into a side by side highway with strong direction.

Julie and I began to brainstorm and create content for a Challenge to Change program appropriate for middle and high school students. Through Julie's leadership and knowledge, as well as her commitment to Challenge to Change's mission, she birthed A Classroom in Balance.

~ Molly Schreiber
Founder & CEO, Challenge to Change, Inc.

• FOREWORD •
Julie Strittmatter

I originally became an educator because of the profound impact my own teachers had on me during my teen years. During my classroom career, I always kept the mental, emotional, and physical health of my students at the epicenter of my pedagogical practices. I recognized that when students walked into my classroom, I was receiving much more than a brain to be stuffed with academic content. I wanted my students to know that I saw their whole selves, and that I was there to support them in any way they needed, not just in academia.

In my six years in teaching, I always offered some level of Mindfulness to my students when they were in my classroom. However, it was during my 95-Hour Children's Yoga Teacher Training at Challenge to Change that I understood on a much deeper level the impact these practices could have on children. I thought to myself, 'How can I not offer this to my students more exclusively?' Therefore, during what became my last year as a classroom teacher, I dedicated the first five minutes of each class period to Mindfulness exercises.

That year I saw a profound shift in myself and my students. The students were more engaged in academic learning and I spent significantly less time managing behaviors. The classroom culture felt far more inclusive and filled with mutual respect than in any year prior. In addition, I personally felt more at ease throughout the workday and more excited to come to work each day.

Each semester I watched our classroom transform from a place to learn into a place to grow. By being provided a safe space to explore their thoughts, feelings, and identities, my students were able to create stronger bonds with themselves, each other, and also with me, their teacher.

It was during this year that I decided to leave my own classroom and commit my heart to Challenge to Change. I wanted to help spread their mission. I'd realized that Molly and I were cut from the same cloth - we believed in acting on our dreams and following our passion through purpose. While it was heart-wrenching to leave my own classroom, I knew that in aligning with Challenge to Change I could expand my reach far beyond the walls of my classroom and benefit numerous children throughout my community and the world.

This book was created with the intention of recreating the experience I had with my students with other teachers and students. I believe in these practices. I believe in education. I believe in teachers. I believe in students. But mostly, I believe that what we do everyday matters.

This book contains the passion of Challenge to Change Inc. and our whole team of change-makers. It holds the heartbeat of every student I've taught and that Molly has taught. It nurtures immense hope for all who will learn and benefit from these lessons and activities.

~ Julie Strittmatter
Yoga Instructor, Writer, Educator

As you begin your journey with A Classroom in Balance, know that you are a change-maker and you are making a positive difference in our world. Please know that you are supported by Molly, Julie, all of Challenge to Change, and all of the teachers who are making a difference in their classrooms each day. We hope this book will change the way you see your students - how they see themselves - and how they see you.

You are invited to take a moment to close your eyes and feel gratitude for yourself as you begin to create more balance for yourself and others. We are so grateful for you.

Are you ready
to create balance in your classroom?

Mindfulness is the practice of being aware. It is a practice because it is something we have to work at every day. Mindfulness involves being aware of what is going on around you; in your mind, in your physical body, and in your emotional body. Because this practice is so broad, you can do anything mindfully. For example, you can breathe mindfully, eat mindfully, walk mindfully, talk mindfully - you can even use social media mindfully. On the other hand, you can also do all of these things without being mindful or paying attention. Think about how quickly your favorite snack disappears when you are sitting in front of the television and not paying attention to what you are eating. A Classroom in Balance invites you to push the pause button in your classroom to create a meaningful shift. These activities will help you engage with the world in a more intentional way in order to enjoy life more fully.

MINDFULNESS CAN
+ Increase Attention
+ Decrease Stress
+ Improve Mood
+ Improve Overall Health

How to use this book.

This book contains one hundred different Mindfulness activities. These activities can be done in ten minutes or less! We invite you to offer these practices as brain breaks for your students, as a way to begin your class with a mindful minute, or maybe even to read them over the intercom for the entire student body to practice each day. Use them as you see fit! Begin to mindfully create, and sustain, balance in your students' mental, emotional, and physical growth.

Each practice has one or a combination of the following icons:

 Utilizes a physical practice.

 Strengthens emotional muscles like compassion, gratitude, or self-love.

 Offers opportunities to work with our thoughts - both conscious and unconscious thinking.

Any activities that require supplies are marked with a ⭐ icon. Please feel free to modify these as you see fit. For example, some of the exercises invite students to use writing as a reflection. It is up to you if you would like students to have a designated Mindfulness Journal, or if you would like them to write on scratch paper.

SUGGESTED SUPPLIES

+ Student journal designated for these practices or loose leaf paper
+ Writing utensils
+ At least 5 Post-it Notes per student

+ Something to create a classroom Gratitude Jar, such as a mason jar, food container, large cup, small box or bin
+ Timer or stopwatch on your phone

Each activity has been scripted for your convenience, with additional suggestions for teachers written in italics. Feel free to read each activity aloud to your class according to the script, or to modify it in your own words. The important thing is that you find your comfort level administering these activities so that you feel authentic guiding your students towards Mindfulness!

Thank you for allowing us to be a part of your mindful journey.

Day   Choose One Intentional Thought

Your brain has a job, and its job is to think. However, sometimes when your brain clocks in for the day, you find that it is not being very productive or it is struggling with the task at hand. Does anyone know how many thoughts you have per day?

Ask for a few answers.

On average, you have **50,000** thoughts every day. Your thoughts begin the moment you wake up, and they don't stop until the moment you go to sleep. Sometimes they even wake us up at night. One of the most beneficial Mindfulness practices you can do is becoming aware of your thoughts. This is because most of the thoughts that go through your mind are negative. Roughly 80% of our thoughts are negative, and over 90% of those thoughts are repetitive. Think about the first thought you had this morning: Is it a thought you would choose to have again tomorrow morning? Or think about the last thought you had before class started. Do you want to think that thought again? You have more power over your mind than it has over you. We can use mindfulness as a tool to help our minds work with us instead of against us. For your first day of Mindfulness, you are invited to choose one intentional thought for the day. What is one thought you would like to have today? Write this down somewhere you will see it.

EXAMPLES:

"I can do hard things."

"Today is a good day."

"I am supported."

"I am grateful for what I have."

"I am enough; I have unlimited potential."

Day **2** Choose Your Thoughts for the Day

This activity involves the use of paper/journal and a writing utensil.
Instruct students to take out their papers and writing utensils.

Mindfulness reminds us that we can choose our thoughts for the day the same way we choose our clothes, what we eat, and the music that we listen to. It is important to deliberately choose our thoughts because, just like our most listened to songs, our thoughts become habits that often replay over and over again in our minds.

I am going to give you five typical scenarios that you likely encounter on a daily basis. Your challenge is to come up with the intentional thoughts you would like to have during each of these moments.

There are very few rules with this; only that your thoughts must be INTENTIONAL and they must be POSITIVE. When each of these moments comes up in your day, pause and remember the thoughts that you chose to have in these circumstances.

If one of these moments passes without you remembering to pause and think your chosen thoughts, it is okay. Just try and remember to think your thoughts the next time that event occurs. Learning to be mindful takes time. This is a practice for us all, and we have to work at it every day.

Please write your intentional thought for each of the following activities:
• Eating your next meal: _____

• Looking in the mirror: _____

• Leaving school for the day: _____

• Walking into your house: _____

• Before you fall asleep: _____

Offer students EXAMPLES:

Eating your next meal...
I am grateful for food that keeps me healthy and nourished.

Looking in the mirror...
I love my eye color.

Leaving school for the day...
I did the best I could today.

Walking into your house...
I am so glad to see my dog.

Before you fall asleep...
I am allowed to relax and go to sleep.

Day 3   Noticing Your Thoughts

This activity involves the use of paper/journal and a writing utensil.
Instruct students to take out their papers and writing utensils.

Noticing our thoughts, or becoming aware of our thinking, is really challenging for most people. However, we can't change something unless we become aware of it. This is important because sometimes we have negative thoughts when we face a challenging moment. For example, if you didn't make the sports team you tried out for, or someone else was chosen for the role you wanted in the school play, it would be completely natural to experience disappointment and think about these events negatively.

Thoughts about tough topics are sometimes uncomfortable, and we often avoid thinking about them at all. However, thinking about the hard things in our lives is very important because it is one of the ways we work through and move past them.

When thinking about uncomfortable situations, we often create judgements and stories around them. This is usually where negative self-talk comes in. Was there a time today when you thought about something difficult and felt negative? Let's use that time to practice being kind to yourself. Maybe someone else was chosen for a job you wanted and you felt hurt and resentful. Rather than focus on the outcome, you can tell yourself they were the right fit for the job and there will be a better opportunity coming your way. This is a practice of not taking events personally. In doing this, we do not create a "story" around why we were not chosen, and instead, look at the facts of the situation. Find a way to build positivity into your thinking during challenging times rather than falling back on doubting yourself.

In your journals, write down at least five thoughts you had today. Those thoughts could be either positive or negative, meaningful or silly. You might want to start with thoughts you had at the beginning of your day, and then work your way sequentially up to the present moment. Take the time to think clearly about all that went through your mind today.

Allow time for students to complete their lists.

Please place a star next to positive thoughts you would choose to have again tomorrow. Then, cross out the thoughts that were not productive, and rewrite these to show kinder and more supportive thoughts.

We now know that our minds are always thinking, and that we can choose whether we are going to have positive or negative thoughts. Sometimes, though, it seems impossible to get our minds to slow down enough for us to process our thoughts.

Over the last few days we practiced ways to think more positively. Over the next few days, we will learn to use breathing techniques to help calm the mind and the body so that we can listen to our thoughts more effectively.

Today we will set ourselves up for a seated practice. Most of us walk around throughout the day with poor posture, and we are unaware of the effect this has on how we feel in our bodies.

Take a moment right now to notice how you are sitting. Uncross your legs, push both feet onto the floor beneath you, and straighten your back. Make some small circles with your shoulders by bringing them up toward your ears and then back down. Sit up tall and proud. You may choose to either close your eyes or look down softly at the ground. We do this because our goal is to calm the mind, and we want to eliminate any distractions from our line of vision. Give yourself permission to just be here right now.

Pause for 30 seconds.

Now take a deep breath in through your nose, and back out through your nose. Repeat this two more times. Breathe in through your nose, and out through your nose. Once more; breathe in deeply, and exhale fully.

Pause for 30 seconds.

Now open your eyes and notice how you feel.

Maybe you feel a little bit calmer, or maybe more alert. It is important to find this seat each time we come into our seated practice because it allows your diaphragm to expand and contract completely. This pulls in more oxygen for our minds and bodies.

Moving forward, notice how you tend to sit throughout your day. In each of your classes, or maybe after school, find this posture from our seated practice and take at least one mindful, deep breath in through your nose and out through your nose. Notice how this makes you feel.

Day   Clearing Your Mind with Counting Breaths

Today we are going to practice a breathing technique that utilizes counting to help us slow our minds and bring us clarity. This breathing technique is incredibly effective because it gives the mind something simple to focus on (counting) while calming the body with the use of the breath. In this breathing practice, we will inhale for a count of three and exhale for a count of three.

Begin by settling your body and finding your seat. Sit with your back against your chair and uncross your ankles. Place your feet flat on the floor. Notice what it feels like to have a tall, proud posture.

Roll your shoulders down your back and away from your ears. Choose to either close your eyes, or take your gaze to the ground. Allow your mind to focus just on your inhales and exhales; counting in your mind as I count out loud. Take a deep breath in through your nose, and back out through your nose.

Inhale 1-2-3, Exhale 3-2-1
Inhale 1-2-3, Exhale 3-2-1
Inhale 1-2-3, Exhale 3-2-1
Inhale 1-2-3, Exhale 3-2-1
Inhale 1-2-3, Exhale 3-2-1
Inhale 1-2-3, Exhale 3-2-1

Open your eyes and notice how you feel.

You may ask for students to share if they notice anything different in themselves after breathing this way. This can be done with a partner or through a whole class discussion.

Day 6 — Triangle Breathing

Today we will learn how to do Triangle Breathing. This activity takes the practice of counting your breaths as you breathe a step further by adding the step of breath retention. Adding breath retention (holding your breath) helps focus your brain even more.

Triangle Breathing looks like this: Inhale 1-2-3; Hold 1-2-3; Exhale 1-2-3. Slowing down each part of the breathing process helps us to calm our minds, bodies, and emotions. You are welcome to do this activity with your eyes open while tracing a triangle on the desk in front of you, or you can do this with your eyes closed.

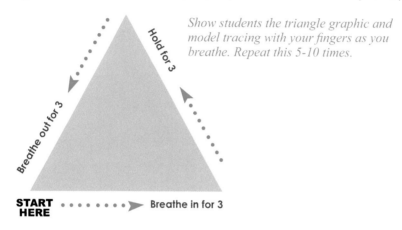

Show students the triangle graphic and model tracing with your fingers as you breathe. Repeat this 5-10 times.

Day 7 — Positive Affirmations

Your mind is a powerful place, and you have the ability to train it to become stronger and more positive. One of the ways you can do this is by putting your attention on your breath, just as we did in Triangle Breathing. Another way you can do this is through positive affirmations or mantras.

Mantras are three word sentences that begin with "I am" and end with a positive word or statement. Examples of mantras include "I am kind", "I am strong", "I am smart", and "I am beautiful".

A positive affirmation can be something you know you already are, or it can be something that you are working toward becoming. What are some positive things you can say about yourself or to a friend? Come up with your own positive affirmation and write it down somewhere you will see it at least three more times today.

Day 8 Mantra Breathing

Positive affirmations are good thoughts we can offer ourselves whenever we want or need a boost in morale. We can tell ourselves a positive affirmation when we are doubting ourselves - like right before we have to present something to the class - and need some extra support. We also can tell ourselves a positive affirmation when we are really proud of ourselves and our accomplishments and want to celebrate our success. Positive affirmations not only help increase our confidence and boost our mood, they can also be tools to help us focus our minds and calm our bodies.

Today we are going to connect our counting breaths of Inhale 1-2-3, Exhale 3-2-1 with a positive affirmation. Find your comfortable seated position with a tall spine and your feet pressing against the floor. Close your eyes or take your gaze to the ground. Let's start with counting breaths:

Inhale 1-2-3, Exhale 3-2-1
Inhale 1-2-3, Exhale 3-2-1
Inhale 1-2-3, Exhale 3-2-1

Now let's replace the numbers with affirmations:

Inhale I-Am-Kind, Exhale I-Am-Kind
Inhale I-Am-Smart, Exhale I-Am-Smart
Inhale I-Am-Strong, Exhale I-Am-Strong
Inhale I-Am-Worthy, Exhale I-Am-Worthy

For the next two breaths repeat this affirmation breathing using your own positive word:

Pause

Take a deep breath in,
Take a deep breath out,
And open your eyes.

Day

Tune In to How You Feel

This activity involves the use of paper/journal and a writing utensil.
Instruct students to take out their papers and writing utensils.

Mindfulness offers you different ways to interact with the world more intentionally. When we pay close attention to how we move and act in the world, it increases our overall happiness, focus, and quality of life.

Part of living more mindfully is paying closer attention to our feelings and emotions. This is because our needs are closely connected to our feelings. Today you will practice tuning in to how you feel.

Take out a piece of paper and fold it in half lengthwise in order to create two columns. Along the sides of both columns write 1, 2, and 3. In the left side column, answer the following questions:

Next to the number 1: **How do I feel mentally?**
Possible answers might be focused, energized, or distracted.

Next to the number 2, answer: **How do I feel emotionally?**
Possible answers might be happy, grateful, annoyed, sad, scared, anxious, or content.

Next to the number 3, answer: **How does my body feel?**
Maybe it is feeling strong, alert, awake, tired, sore, or tight.

Offer students time to answer these questions in the left column of their paper.

We will now practice six rounds of Triangle Breathing to determine if anything shifts in the way we feel in our minds, bodies, and emotions after we engage in this breath practice.

Lead students through six rounds of Triangle Breathing from Day 6.

Now that we have engaged in Triangle Breathing, please answer those same three questions on the right side of your paper. Be thoughtful in reflecting on any changes that took place inside yourself after engaging in this practice. Maybe you notice that your mind feels more calm, or you are more focused. Perhaps you don't notice any changes at all. There are no right or wrong answers here.

OPTIONAL: Allow students to share their changes with a partner or as a whole class discussion.

1• How do I feel mentally?	1• How do I feel mentally?
2• How do I feel emotionally?	2• How do I feel emotionally?
3• How does my body feel?	3• How does my body feel?

· · · · · · · **10** ·

Day Watching Your Thoughts Like Clouds in the Sky

Yesterday we explored checking in with our minds, bodies, and emotions. Maybe you have noticed that the way you feel - whether mentally, physically, or emotionally - changes day by day, and sometimes even minute by minute. Sometimes our thoughts and feelings change so quickly that we do not even notice that they are there. However, there are also times when it seems that what we are feeling is going to last forever. For example, when we are really happy, it is hard to remember a time when we were sad. Conversely, when we are feeling hopeless, it is hard to believe that we will ever feel happy again. Today's Mindfulness activity helps us to watch our thoughts and feelings and to remember that none of them are permanent.

Sit quietly and calmly in your seated position. During this practice, I invite you to close your eyes to help you use your imagination for a guided visualization of your thoughts. Imagine in your mind's eye that you can see a beautiful, blue sky in front of you. You can feel the warmth of the sun, and maybe even smell the flowers of a spring day.

This sky represents your mind. When the sky is clear, so is your mind - there are no thoughts passing through. However, it is very challenging to have a clear mind all the time. As you sit here today, notice when a thought comes into your mind, and try to see it as a cloud passing through the sky. Rather than focus on the cloud or allow it to become a dark gray storm cloud, just let it come into your mind then let it pass, just like white fluffy clouds rolling through the sky on a windy day. Do your best to watch these thoughts roll in and out, in and out, without judging yourself for them. I will be silent for the next minute.

Allow one minute in silence.

Now slowly bring your attention back to your breathing. Take three deep breaths in and out and notice how your mind feels. Open your eyes.

Day   Inner Critic vs. Inner Best Friend

Inside your mind you have two voices narrating your internal dialogue. One of them is your Inner Critic, and the other is your Inner Best Friend. They both have a lot to say, but you have to decide whom you want to hand the microphone to in your mind.

Let's say you are taking a math test. You have prepared for it, but you do not fully understand the content. You are on question five when you notice that others around you are already on another page. If you hand your Inner Critic the microphone, it might say something like, "You are not smart enough to be in this class." or, "Of course you are behind, you are always behind."

On the other hand, your Inner Best Friend might say, "It's okay that they are on the next page and you aren't yet. Take your time and slow down. Don't focus on what anyone else is doing." Or it might say, "All you can do is your best. Remember what you studied, and that you do not have to be perfect at everything."

If you were having a bad day, you would probably choose to call your best friend to cheer you up, not someone who picks on you or is mean to you. Likewise, in times of stress, learn to turn to your Inner Best Friend and tune your Inner Critic out.

Before you can really rely on your Inner Best Friend, though, you first have to learn to watch your thoughts like you did yesterday; watch them pass through your mind like clouds in the sky. Once you become aware of them, you can hand the microphone over to your Inner Best Friend.

Let's try this activity together:

SCENARIO: You leave your favorite sweatshirt somewhere in the school and you cannot remember where you put it.

- What might be something your Inner Critic would say?
  Ex: You are so stupid. You always lose things.
- What might be something your Inner Best Friend would say?
  Ex: It is okay. We can retrace our steps to try to find it, and hopefully it will turn up.

SCENARIO: You send a text to one of your friends. You can see that they read it, but they have not responded all day. Nor did they say "Hi" to you in the hallway.

- What might be something your Inner Critic would say?
  Ex: You did something wrong and they do not want to be friends with you anymore.
- What might be something your Inner Best Friend would say?
  Ex: I wonder if they opened it in class and never actually read it. Maybe they have that stressful history test next block and that is all they can think of.

Ask students to come up with their own examples, either writing them down or discussing them with a neighbor.

Day Strengthening Your Inner Best Friend

This activity involves the use of paper/journal and a writing utensil.
Instruct students to take out their papers and writing utensils.

The goal of today is to strengthen your Inner Best Friend. This might seem counterintuitive, but in order to do this, you must first listen to your Inner Critic. We cannot change our negative thought patterns if we are not aware of them.

Take a moment to write down some of the thoughts that you have about yourself, whether positive or negative. Some things to consider: What are your thoughts about your own intelligence? What are your thoughts about your physical appearance? What are your thoughts about yourself as a friend and/or a family member?

Allow students to reflect on these in their journals.

Looking at your thoughts, would you allow a friend to talk about you that way? Would you talk about a friend that way? If the answer is no, those are the thoughts that are unproductive. This does not mean we cannot look at our behaviors and wish to improve upon them. What it means is it's unproductive for us to be mean to ourselves. We can absolutely work to better ourselves, but we do not need to be cruel to ourselves in order to do so. The next time you notice one of these thoughts come into your mind, give yourself the same advice you would give your own best friend if they said those things to themselves.

day Write a Positive Affirmation on the Board

Put out various dry erase markers or pieces of chalk, depending if you have a whiteboard or chalkboard in your classroom. You can also do this activity on a piece of poster paper if you prefer. Before the activity begins, please write your own "I Am" statement(s) on the board for the students to see. If possible, leave the statements produced during this activity on the board for the remainder of class.

Choose a positive "I Am" Statement for the day and write it on the board. Remember, this can be something you know you are, or something you would like to become. "I Am _____" Your "I Am" statement could be something like:

I Am Unique, I Am Talented, I Am Peaceful, I Am Loved, I Am Beautiful, I Am Trying

Have students take turns reading their "I Am" statements out loud to the class. Option to have students orally explain why they are that mantra. For example, "I am proud because I got a B on my science project."

Who remembers how many thoughts we have per day?

Take a few answers.

50,000 -80,000

Who remembers how many of those thoughts are negative?

Take a few answers.

80%

Why do you think we use positive affirmations?

Take a few answers.

When we have negative thoughts about ourselves, it has a domino effect on our overall mood, confidence, and motivation. When our mood is lowered, our confidence is lowered, and our motivation is lowered. It is not likely we will be very successful at anything that we partake in if we have a pessimistic attitude.

To counter our inclination to think negatively, we can use positive affirmations. Positive affirmations help train our brains to believe the good about ourselves. Everyone doubts themselves sometimes--even your favorite celebrity, best friend, and your parents.

Today, your Mindfulness mission is to ask someone in your life to share a positive affirmation. You might need to give them some examples that they can use. Perhaps you can share with them why positive affirmations are important, as well as some of your favorites "I Am" statements.

Day   Concentrating the Mind

Today's practice centers on focusing the mind. Focus is something that most of us struggle with from time to time, as it can be challenging to be fully present and to only focus on one task at a time.

Sometimes we become distracted because we are thinking of something that happened in the past, or we are thinking of something that might happen in the future. In other words, our minds can travel anywhere other than the present, and this prevents us from being fully focused on the here and now.

Begin by finding your comfortable seat from our seated practice. Plant your feet on the ground, push your back against your chair, and sit up tall and proud. Lower your shoulders away from your ears and relax your jaw.

Keep your eyes open, but focus your attention to one item on the ground that is not moving. Do your best to look only at this point throughout our practice. You might be surprised by how many times your mind instinctually wants you to look away from this spot - keeping your eyes on this spot will remind you to stay tuned in to our practice. Keep your eyes focused while turning your attention to the breath.

Inhale 1-2-3, Exhale 3-2-1
Inhale 1-2-3, Exhale 3-2-1
Inhale 1-2-3, Exhale 3-2-1

You may choose to use your Mantra Breath instead of counting:

Inhale, I am focused.
Exhale, I am focused.

Or you might choose to simply sit and breathe.

Allow thirty seconds for students to choose their practice.

Remember that your brain's job is to think, and your wandering mind is proof that your brain is trying to do its job right now. When your mind wanders, try to bring your attention back to your breath and that one spot on the ground.

Allow thirty seconds to one minute to practice.

When you are ready, take one more full breath in, and a full breath out. Know that anytime you are struggling to focus, you can bring your eyes to one spot and breathe. Notice everything you can about your breath for a few minutes.

Finish with one to two more minutes of quiet breathing.

Day MOUNTAIN POSE:
Setting Yourself Up for Standing Practice

Just like we set ourselves up for success in a seated practice, we are going to set ourselves up for success in a standing practice by learning Mountain Pose. Begin by standing up naturally. Notice how you normally stand. Notice this without any judgement about yourself, just with awareness.

Follow these subtle cues to find Mountain Pose: Place your feet under your hips and soften your knees so they are not locked. Stand up taller, allowing the top of your head to reach up toward the ceiling. Roll your shoulders away from your ears and soften the muscles in your face. Allow your arms to rest by your side and reach your fingertips toward the floor.

You might notice how rarely you stand like this. Mountain Pose is named after mountains because they are tall, strong, stable, silent, and proud. Try to envision yourself as a mountain. This is the foundation for all standing poses, and even for activities like running and jumping. Now, close your eyes. Notice if your body begins to sway a bit side to side. Do your best to keep yourself balanced.

Take a deep breath in,
and a deep breath out.
Inhale and think, "I am balanced."
Exhale and think, "I am balanced."
Inhale, "I am stable."
Exhale, "I am stable."

Notice how it feels to stand tall and proud.
You can return here anytime you need in your day without anyone knowing what you are doing.

Day

Concentrating Breath Practice; Tippy Toe Breath

Today we will continue to enhance our concentration by adding body movements to our breathing. If you would like to take your shoes off for today's practice, you may. Being barefoot might help you better connect your movement with your breath.

Begin by standing in Mountain Pose with your feet underneath your hips. Stand with a tall spine, open heart, and relaxed shoulders. In your Mountain Pose, find something on the ground that is not moving to focus your eyes. Keep your eyes glued there as we do Tippy Toe Breathing.

Inhale and come up onto your tippy toes. Pause briefly at the top. Exhale and roll onto the balls of your feet, allowing your toes to come off of the floor just a little bit. You may notice that you wobble a bit here; that is completely normal. Continue to inhale, coming up onto your tippy toes, and as you exhale, roll onto the balls of your feet, letting your toes come slightly off of the floor.

Options: If you are feeling a little off balance today, keep one, or both, hands on a desk or chair in front of you. If you are feeling extra balanced and centered, you can choose to close your eyes while you do your Tippy Toe Breath. Remember, this is a type of breath and movement practice that requires concentration, so do your best to only think of what you are doing right now.

Over the last two days we explored techniques for improving our focus. Today, we will use balancing yoga poses to help focus our minds even more.

Balancing yoga poses improve our focus because they require all of our attention in order to stay upright. It is challenging to think about what you are going to eat for dinner while also standing on one leg.

Begin by coming into your Mountain Pose. Stand up tall and proud. Place your feet underneath your hips and bring your hands to your hips. Keeping your spine as tall as you can, shift your weight into your left leg. Pull your right knee up and in toward your chest at a ninety-degree angle. Flex the foot as though you are going to put it on the floor or on a chair in front of you.

Remember to keep your gaze on a point in front of you that is not moving to help you stay balanced. Slowly lower the right leg. Take a deep breath in and out while standing in your Mountain Pose, and then shift the weight into your right leg. Keeping your spine tall, pull the left knee up and in toward your chest. Feel your lower belly strength support you. Take a deep breath in and out. Lower the leg down. Repeat this three times.

For an added challenge, see if you can extend the lifted leg straight out in front of you to make it parallel with the floor.

Day Challenging Balancing and Focus

The mind is like any other muscle in the body; it gets stronger the more it is worked. The more challenging you make your workouts, the more is required of your body to build strength. The mind works the same way; the more of a mental challenge you give it, the stronger it gets.

We can make any activity easier or more challenging based on our wants and needs for the day. Remember that this is your practice, and it is not for anyone else. Do not worry about what someone next to you is doing. Do what feels right for you.

We are going to challenge the mind and body simultaneously. Begin in Mountain Pose. Feel your feet connected to the earth. Take a moment to find your focal point; remember this is one point that does not move. Take a deep breath in and out.

Shift your weight into your left leg and begin to bring your right knee up and in toward your chest. You can have your hands on your hips, by your side, or bring your palms to touch at your heart center. If you would like to keep your eyes glued on your focal point, please do so.

If you want more of a challenge, see if you can bring your gaze up to the place where the wall meets the ceiling. Just be mindful of how that changes your balance. If you would like even more of a challenge, see if you can close your eyes while keeping your balance.

Remember to breathe. Then slowly lower your leg. Repeat this practice on the other side by beginning in your Mountain Pose with your eyes glued to your focal point. Decide if you want to look up, straight ahead at your focal point, or if you want to close your eyes. Remember to breathe, keeping your shoulders relaxed with a tall spine.

Give a few moments for students to reflect if their balance was easier or harder without one thing to focus on.

Day 20 Refocusing the Wandering Mind

It is completely natural for our minds to wander and think about things other than what is right in front of us. However, this can be frustrating and cause stress when we want to be focused and calm.

We have been working on keeping our gaze on one point to help focus the mind. Today we are going to practice using our breath to help refocus our minds when they start to wander.

Begin by finding your seated posture with a tall spine. Close your eyes and take a deep inhale and exhale. Notice what it feels like to sit in stillness and in silence. Notice how your mind feels today. Do your best to notice this without any judgement. Have you been focused? Is there something that has been pulling your attention? Does your brain feel like a computer with too many tabs open? Whatever it feels like, it is okay. We are going to give our full attention today to the breath.

As you inhale, notice how your belly slowly rises as the air gently moves into your chest. Recognize that when you exhale, the breath leaves your chest first and then your belly. Inhale, feel the belly and chest expand. Exhale, feel the chest and belly fall.

Maybe you can watch your breath so closely that you even notice the beginning of your inhale and follow it all the way to its peak. Notice the small, natural pause that happens just before the exhale, and follow your exhale all the way to its completion. Repeat this.

Inhale, notice as the breath draws in, and follow it until you reach the height of your inhale. Pause, then notice the breath as it releases. Sit in silence for the next few moments with your attention on the breath. If your mind wanders, that is natural. Just gently bring your awareness back to your breath.

Pause for thirty seconds.

Notice if your mind has drifted off with thoughts. Gently bring your awareness back to your inhales and exhales.

Pause for one minute.

If your mind is elsewhere, come back to right here, right now. Let's all take one more deep, intentional breath together; in through the nose, and out through the nose. When you are ready, open your eyes.

Ask students how long they think they paused for in silence the second time. Facilitate a discussion with them about how time slows down when we pay attention.

Do you remember the definition of Mindfulness?

Take a few examples.

mindfulness is...
+ being conscious or aware
+ being present with what is going on and being non-judgemental
+ paying attention to our thoughts and feelings

Mindfulness takes on many forms. We can eat mindfully, walk mindfully, or speak mindfully. We have the power to do anything we want to with mindful intention. Sometimes Mindfulness practices are done sitting down and quieting the mind. Other times, Mindfulness is found through movement like yoga poses. Still other times Mindfulness is studying how we think and what we think about. From now on, our Mindfulness practices are going to begin integrating questions to encourage reflection and growth. Remember that there are no right or wrong answers to these questions.

Ask students to come up with their own definitions of Mindfulness in their journals. Offer them enough time to reflect on their most and least favorite Mindfulness activities they have practiced, with reasons why they have or have not enjoyed them. They are welcome to decorate these pages as they see fit. Feel free to bring out colored pencils or markers for them to decorate.

This activity involves the use of paper/journal and a writing utensil.
Instruct students to take out their papers and writing utensils.

Instruct students to write their first names at the top of their papers.

When we are used to doing something, it becomes like second nature to us. Think about tying your shoes, brushing your teeth, walking the path from the kitchen to your bedroom, or answering a phone. These are all actions that come naturally to you because you have done them countless times. These are also the activities our brain goes into autopilot while doing, and we become very unpresent, unaware, and mindless while doing them.

Did you have to concentrate when you wrote your name at the top of the paper? It is likely you did not have to think very hard while you wrote it, and you possibly do not fully remember even writing it. Let's try this again, write your name at the top of your paper without allowing your pen or pencil to come off of the paper. This will require a bit more of your attention than writing your name normally.

Allow time for students to write without taking the pen off of the page.

Continue to instruct students to write their name using the following modifications:
+ with their eyes closed
+ using their left hand
+ beginning with the last letter and working their way back

Becoming aware of what we are doing is called Mindfulness. It is normal for us to go into autopilot from time to time when we do activities that we have mastered, but we also have the power to be fully aware while we participate in any and all activities.

Allow a few moments for student reflection in their journals, or facilitate a group conversation about the thought processes involved when doing something that is new and different. Perhaps ask your students what other activities they tend to do on autopilot, and how they might practice these activities more mindfully in the future.

Day Mindful Walk

This activity invites you to take students out of the classroom. It can take place in the hallway or outside if the weather and time permit.

Instruct students to stand up and take five steps and stop.

Walking is another activity we do on a daily basis. We do not need to think much about what we are doing when we are walking from one place to the next. Walking mindfully differs from everyday walking because you pay attention to slowly putting one foot in front of the other while carefully listening to and watching all that is happening around you.

Instruct students to be more mindful as they walk back to where they began.

Taking a quiet walk is an amazing Mindfulness practice that can be added to just about any day! Taking a Mindfulness walk is quite simple: All you need to do is be silent, pay attention to what you hear, and walk at a calm pace.

Walking mindfully means you are aware of what is going on around you. It invites you to be mindful of the people around you, the sounds around you, and the thoughts within you. We are going to go to *(your chosen location)* for a Mindful Walk.

During our Mindful Walk, please do not make eye contact with anyone around you, and please remain silent. Your invitation during this walk is to listen to the sounds around you, and notice the thoughts you have. Be mindful of all of the sounds that exist around you with each step that you take.

Take students to the chosen location and allow them to walk for one to three minutes.

Day Encouraging Yourself and Others

This week, we were reminded that when we repeat activities like walking, they become easier. Sometimes daily activities become so easy that we do not have to think about them at all; we begin to do them on autopilot.

On the other hand, when we are learning something new, we have to think very carefully about each step because we do not know how to do it efficiently yet.

Mindfulness can be applied to skills we have mastered to help us to stay present during the task, and to learning completely new skills in order to increase our focus and our patience with ourselves.

Think about the last time you tried something new. Maybe it was when you wrote your name with your eyes closed. Maybe it was something new you did in science class, or maybe it was helping someone at home with a task. Can you recall your thoughts? Did you hear your Inner Best Friend, or did you hear your Inner Critic? It is normal for us to have negative self-talk when we are learning something new. Just because it is normal, though, it does not mean it is helpful to us.

What words of encouragement can you say to yourself when you are learning something new? Can you think of words of encouragement you offered a friend when they were trying to learn a new skill?

Ask each student to come up with an example of what they can say to themselves when they are learning something new. Take a response from each student. Challenge students to remember these positive phrases they can say while learning something new throughout the week.

Day Working with Nonjudgement

As much as Mindfulness is about constant awareness, it is also about being non-judgemental. Today's practice is about being aware of our thoughts and being accepting of them, even when they are not thoughts we want to have.

Come into your posture for a seated practice. Remember to sit in an alert position with a tall spine. Take a deep breath to sit tall, but with ease. It can be helpful to think about lengthening your spine while also softening your shoulders and the muscles of your face. Take another deep breath in, and then let it go completely. Close your eyes and do this twice more.

Pause for the two breaths.

Allow your breath to return to normal. Begin by checking in with yourself. Notice how your mind feels today. Notice what thoughts are going through your mind. Notice if you are judging yourself for the thoughts you are having. Mindfulness is more than just this awareness; it is also about generating kindness and compassion for ourselves.

It is especially important to be patient with yourself when you notice that your mind is thinking about things other than what you want it to focus on, or when you are thinking negative thoughts about yourself when you are trying to be positive. When you find your mind doing this, you can simply bring your focus back to your breathing to recenter yourself on the present moment and on the positive.

During practice today, I will be quiet for thirty second increments, and then I will remind you to breathe. When you hear my voice, notice if your mind is somewhere else. If it is, see if you can be nonjudgmental toward yourself and gently bring it back to this moment. Allow your breath to remain natural to you and use it as a focal point for your mind.

Pause for thirty seconds.

"Breathe."

Repeat this three more times.

If you notice that your mind has been other places, remember that this is normal and gently bring your attention back to your breath. Be aware of the thoughts you are creating around your own thinking, or notice if you aren't really having any thoughts at all right now. Just let yourself be.

Pause for thirty seconds.

"Breathe."

Repeat this three more times.

Gently open your eyes and notice how you feel.

Day Setting Yourself up for a Yoga Nap

Over the last few days, you have been invited to bring a new awareness to familiar activities that you are used to doing. Today we are going to try something new and get ourselves set up for a Yoga Nap. A Yoga Nap is not like a regular nap, as the goal is not to fall asleep. Instead, the goal is to relax the body and mind, just like we do in our seated practice. This time, however, we will be lying down.

If you are uncomfortable lying down and you would prefer to do this practice in a seated position, you are welcome to do so. Please keep in mind that there are benefits to both positions.

Your body and your mind are so connected. Sometimes in order for the mind to relax, the body needs to be relaxed first. Other times, in order for us to relax the body, we must begin with the mind. The Yoga Nap helps both your body and mind to connect and relax to deepen your experience of Mindfulness.

In a moment, you will find a space to lie down on the floor. Please be sure this is a clear, open space without anything overhead. Be careful that you are not touching anyone else. It is important that you find a space where you will not be distracted by friends you might wish to talk with.

Instruct students to find their spots for a Yoga Nap. Redirect students as you see fit.

In your space, lie down on your back with your arms either by your side or on your belly. Allow both legs to extend long. Uncross them if they are crossed. Maybe you can create space between your shoulders and your ears; and maybe you turn your hands palms up to relax your shoulders further. You are safe here; there is nothing you need to worry about.

Remember that new things often feel uncomfortable, both mentally and physically. If this feels uncomfortable to you right now, that is okay - just be willing to open yourself up to something new. If you are comfortable doing so, close your eyes.

Let's all take a full breath in and a full breath out. We will not stay here for very long today; the goal is for you to get comfortable in this posture, and we will revisit it later. When you come into this pose, your only goal is to relax. There is nothing else that you need to do here, absolutely nothing. Can you give yourself permission to stop "doing" right now? Permission to not check your phone, to not give in to your thoughts? Permission to just be?

We are going to take five deep breaths in this space today. Keep your eyes closed as I guide you through the breath.

Inhale *(count to three mentally)*, Exhale *(count to three mentally)*
Repeat this four more times.

Slowly begin to move in just your fingers, and then move in your fingers and toes. Notice what it feels like to be in a relaxed body. Remember that this feeling is always available to you. Let your stretches become larger, maybe reaching the fingers away from the toes, maybe pulling the knees into the chest for a hug. Slowly roll onto one side, and gently come up into a comfortable seat.

Day 27   Body Scan

Today we will use a guided Mindfulness practice called a Body Scan. In a Body Scan, you work to relax one part of the body at a time in order to promote a feeling of overall relaxation and well-being. This practice is incredibly beneficial when we are experiencing stress, anxiety, having a hard time falling asleep, or just want to unwind at the end of the day. This practice can be done seated, but it is most commonly practiced lying down, just like in the position you found yesterday.

Instruct students to return to their space from yesterday's practice, but also give them the option to stay seated if they prefer.

Lie down on your back. Extend your arms long by your side, and reach your legs long while letting your feet fall apart naturally. Take a long deep inhale, followed by a long, deep exhale. Allow your eyes to close, and notice if there are places in your body that you can soften.

As we begin our Body Scan, remember to take deep breaths, and to keep bringing your awareness back to your body without judgement when your mind wanders. Remember you are safe and that this is your time to relax from the stress of your day.

Read the following at a slow and mindful pace. Watch the students to help your pacing, and add any other specific cues you see they might need.

- Bring your attention to the top of your head.
- Unwrinkle your forehead by relaxing all the muscles above your eyebrows.
- Soften through your jaw; let your tongue release off the roof of your mouth.
- Relax your neck, the sides of your neck, the back of your neck, and your throat.
- Let your shoulders blades separate from each other.
- Feel this relaxation begin to move down your arms, forearms, palms, and out each fingertip.
- Remember to take deep breaths.
- Feel a softness through your chest.
- Soften your abdomen and feel the breath move in and out as you inhale and exhale.
- Loosen the muscles of your back, feeling this relaxation move down along your spine.
- Take a breath in and out while thinking about softening the muscles of your lower back.
- Dissolve any tension you've been holding in your hips; let them relax completely into the earth.
- Soften through the upper thighs.
- Release any gripping in the lower legs.
- Allow your ankles to fall apart naturally.
- Feel ease move out of your ankles, the tops of your feet, the bottoms of your feet, and over each toe.
- Take three deep breaths here, noticing if there is anywhere in your body you can soften even more.
- Notice how it feels to take time to quiet the body and the mind.
- Know that this feeling of relaxation is always available to you.
- Begin to wiggle your fingers and toes to bring small movement back into a relaxed body.
- Allow your stretches to become larger and move in any way you need.
- Pull your knees into your chest, gently roll onto one side, and bring yourself up into a comfortable seat.

Day Mantra Breath

We are going to find another way to connect our mantras, or positive affirmations, with our breathing today. Come into your posture for seated practice with a tall spine and relaxed shape. Begin by placing your hand over your heart. We are going to use soft tapping of our hands against our chest to help increase the connection of our positive thoughts with our calm bodies.

Let students know you will demonstrate this and then they will join in. Tap your hand against your heart gently, one tap for each word.

I *(tap)*
Am *(tap)*
Calm *(tap)*

Let's all try this together three times saying the phrases out loud while tapping.
I *(tap)*
Am *(tap)*
Calm *(tap)*
Repeat two more times.

Now, let's try this in a whisper.
I *(tap)*
Am *(tap)*
Calm *(tap)*
Repeat two more times.

Now let's try this just thinking the phrases in our minds.
(tap)
(tap)
(tap)
Repeat two more times.

Now, do not tap your heart, but still think these phrases in your mind two more times as you breathe.

There is a lot of power when a room full of people can share the same positive thought, even if they do not say it out loud. Maybe you could sense that those around you were having the same thought as you. I know I could, and it made me feel connected and at peace. Did any of you feel this way too?

Day 29   Mantra Walk

This activity involves the use of paper/journal and a writing utensil.
Instruct students to take out their papers and writing utensils.

Today we will combine mantras with a Mindfulness Walk. To do this, please begin by writing five of your favorite positive affirmations on your paper. Remember, a positive affirmation is something that we know we are, or something positive we want to become. Examples are, "I Am Enough", "I Am Creative", "I Am Sensitive", "I Am Fearless", and "I Am Unique".

Wait until students have their five examples. Students are going to walk towards the front of the room, taking five mindful steps while thinking their positive affirmation in their minds. They will then repeat this on their way back to their seats. Use your judgment with where you would like for them to stand to begin their mindful walk, and make adaptations as needed.

Please stand. You can bring your papers with you if you would like, or if you are confident you will remember your phrases, feel free to keep them at your desk. From your space, you will take five mindful steps while thinking about your positive affirmations with each step. To take a mindful step, really think about allowing your heel to touch the earth, and then rolling onto the ball of your foot. Allow your foot to plant completely before you pick up your other foot to take another step forward. These steps will be slow, silent, and you will repeat one affirmation for each step.

Demonstrate a slow, mindful step while saying your affirmation out loud.

You will do this for five steps. Challenge yourself to see how slowly you can move, and when your five steps are complete, repeat this exercise on your way back to your seat.

When you feel they are ready, allow students to take their five steps with their affirmations, and then instruct them to do the same on the way back.

Day 30 Share a Mantra With a Classmate

Students will need a partner for this activity. Decide if you would like for them to choose their own partners, or if you would like to assign the pairs.

Positive affirmations are a great way for us to boost our own confidence, and they can also be offered to other people as words of encouragement and support. Not only does it feel good to receive a positive affirmation from a friend, classmate, parent, or coach, it also feels really good to give one.

You never know what the person next to you is going through in life, or whether their Inner Critic has the microphone in their mind. The same is true for you; others don't know what life events you might be experiencing or what thoughts are running through your mind. That is why it is always best to be kind.

Today you will get a partner, and you will choose a positive affirmation for that person. It can be one of the affirmations you chose for yourself yesterday, or it can be a new mantra chosen specifically for them.

It might feel uncomfortable at first to say something nice directly to someone else, and it might feel uncomfortable to receive kind words yourself. In our society, we tend to joke around with others a lot, and we often dismiss words of praise from others so that we don't appear arrogant. However, it is important to give and receive kindness, and offering mantras is a great way to do this. Do your best and have fun.

Tell students who their partners will be, or allow them to choose their own. Instruct them to choose a mantra for their partner, and instruct students to sit or stand with their partners if they are not already doing so.

This exercise is simple. Please look at your partner and make eye contact with them. Say a positive statement beginning with the words, "You are." Whoever's name comes first alphabetically will share the affirmation for their partner first.

Day Mantra Yoga Nap

We will continue to explore the theme of positive affirmations today, and we will use them while in our Yoga Naps. A mantra is a phrase you can say over and over to yourself to help you focus your mind and become more positive. In your Yoga Nap today, I will be reading different mantras for you to repeat in your own mind.

Begin by setting yourself up for your Yoga Nap. Find an appropriate space in the room, and allow yourself to completely relax. See if there is anywhere in your body where you can soften, such as your shoulders, your face, or your hips. Take deep inhales and exhales and feel your body begin to calm. Breathe in and out, in and out. Let's connect the breath with a mantra to help us think more positively. After I say each mantra, please repeat it in your mind quietly.

Read these slowly as though practicing the 1-2-3 breaths.

I Am Safe	I Am Expressive
I Am Strong	I Am a Good Listener
I Am Healthy	I Am Respectful
I Am Creative	I Am Unique
I Am Passionate	I Am Wise
I Am Talented	I Am Beautiful
I Am Confident	I Am Amazing
I Am Empowered	I Am Peaceful
I Am Trying	I Am Trustworthy
I Am Compassionate	
I Am Lovable	
I Am Grateful	

Take a moment to repeat the mantra that meant the most to you today in your mind three times.

Pause for three breaths.

Bring a soft smile to your face as you begin to wiggle in your fingers and your toes. Give yourself any gentle stretch that feels good, and then roll onto one side before coming up to a seated position.

Day Getting Rid of Your Worries

*This activity involves the use of paper/journal and a writing utensil.
Instruct students to rip a piece of paper out of their notebooks.*

Today we will toss away our worries. Worrying is a natural part of life. Sometimes we worry because we do not know what will happen in a situation. Sometimes we worry because we care a lot about a person or a project and their well-being. Other times we worry for no reason at all.

To worry, or think about possible outcomes, is normal and potentially helpful in some cases. It would be challenging for us to live with zero worries at all. However, most of the time we spend worrying is wasted energy, as we have the tendency to catastrophize, or imagine the worst.

It can be really helpful to journal or talk with someone about our worries to get them out of our minds. Today we are going to, quite literally, rip our worries to shreds.

On your piece of paper, please write down any worry going through your mind. You might choose to write about something you fear, a sadness that is weighing you down, or an incomplete goal you have. Perhaps you write down the negative self-talk you have been hearing your Inner Critic say to you lately.

You have the opportunity here to write down anything you want to get rid of. Know that nobody else is going to read your paper; this is just for you. When you are finished making your list, you will shred these worries up into pieces and put them in the recycling bin. Please begin to write your worries on your paper.

Give students a few minutes to write their worries.

Look at your list of worries and ask yourself if any of these worries are beneficial to you; meaning, do any of them help you become the best version of you? If so, copy these worries into your journal to save and cross them off your original list. If not, be prepared to let them go.

Look at your remaining worries that aren't helpful to you and think to yourself, "I am ready to let these go."

Whenever you are ready, begin to shred these papers into whatever size pieces you would like. When you are finished, take a nice deep breath in and out, and then silently place the shredded paper in the recycling bin.

Option: If students kept any worries that they viewed as being beneficial to themselves, discuss how they can phrase these in a more positive manner. Example: Change, "I might fail my math test," to, "I need to be sure to study hard for my math test so that I am fully prepared."

Day Windmill Breath

There are tons of ways for us to clear our minds. We can do things like journal, write negative thoughts down and rip them up, take a Yoga Nap, talk to a friend, go for a walk, engage in yoga, or even do breathing practices. We are going to learn a concentrating type of breath practice today that really helps to clear the mind. It is called Windmill Breath. There are a few different ways we can practice Windmill Breath. I will let you try them all to see what feels best for you. Begin by standing in your Mountain Pose. Remember to bring your feet under your hips and stand up nice and tall with a straight spine. Use your abdominal muscles to hold yourself steady.

Relax your shoulders. Inhale and reach your arms in front of you and then up alongside of your ears. Exhale and make a circle backwards with both of your arms to bring them back by your side. Inhale, reach your arms forward and up alongside your ears; exhale, bring your arms behind you and then back down by your sides.

Repeat this twice more with your own breath, feeling the muscles in your shoulders and chest start to open. Inhaling, reach forward and up, and exhaling, reach back and down. Maybe you can even find a focal point that is not moving, just like you did when we learned Tippy-Toe Breath.

Now see what happens if you take your windmill in the opposite direction. Inhaling, reach the arms behind you and then up by your ears, and exhale, allow them to come in front of you and then down by your sides. Repeat this twice more.

We are going to take this one step further, and this really requires all of your focus and attention because we are going to move our arms in opposite directions. Inhale both of your arms alongside your ears. As you exhale, bring one arm forward and one arm backwards. Pause at shoulder height, then keep them moving in the direction they were traveling in. Bring them both by your sides and pause. Now bring the opposite arm forward, opposite arm backwards, and pause at the top. Do this twice very slowly. Start over at the top as many times as you need to as this is a very tricky practice. When you are ready, begin to speed this motion up to see if you can link the windmill movement with the breath. Remember to pay attention to your thoughts about yourself when you are learning something new!

Take a moment to do whichever version of Windmill Breath feels the best for you for three rounds of breath.

Day 34 Warrior Poses

Today we are going to practice three yoga poses that help to strengthen and stretch different muscles in the body. The Warrior yoga poses are some of the most commonly recognized, and they are actually very complex. Just like a warrior, these yoga poses are strong, intentional, and have purpose. When you engage in them, they can help you to feel strong, focused, and purposeful as well. Begin by standing in your Mountain Pose.

WARRIOR ONE

Step your right foot back and put it at a 45-degree angle.
Take your hands to your hips and allow them to face forward directly under your shoulders.
Bend into your front knee, working the knee and ankle toward a 90-degree angle.
Pull your lower belly up and in. This is the center of your strength. Remember this in the next two poses as well.
Reach your arms up alongside of your ears and spread your fingers wide.
Push into the outer edge of your back foot.
If you want to, you can look up in between your hands.
Take a full breath in and a full breath out.

WARRIOR TWO

Straighten your front leg, and open your back foot to bring it from 45-degrees to 90-degrees.
Let your hips open to the side.
Bend back into your front knee and look to see that your knee is tracking over your pinky toe.
Reach your left arm forward and your right arm back.
Pull your shoulder blades in toward one another and soften them away from your ears.
Push energy out of your fingertips.
Look over your front center finger and keep your eyes glued there as you breathe in and breathe out.

PEACEFUL WARRIOR

Keep your lower body just as it is.
Flip your front palm up to the sky and slowly reach it up and back as though you are drawing an arc with your hands.
Let your right hand come onto your back right leg.
Keep the deep bend in your left leg.
Breathe.

Repeat these poses on the other side.

Does anyone know what it means to be grateful?

Take a few responses.

To be grateful means to be thankful: It is showing appreciation for what you have. People who practice gratitude often feel calmer and more peaceful because they recognize how full and complete their lives really are; they don't truly feel the need to collect more and more "things" to feel happy.

It is important to practice expressing gratitude for what we have because it lets others know we appreciate what it is they bring into our lives, and it helps us to have a positive outlook on ourselves. Practicing gratitude has many benefits including strengthening the immune system, increasing optimism, improved sleep patterns, and decreased stress levels.

Take a moment to think of something that you are grateful for. It can be something simple like chocolate chip cookies, cozy sweatshirts, or funny animal videos; or it can be something more serious like having access to clean drinking water, a bed to sleep in at night, or the members of your family. We are going to go around the room once, and each of us will say something that we are grateful for in our lives.

Have students go around the room and each individually share one thing they are grateful for.

Day 36   Warrior, Not Worrier

Today we are going to revisit the three Warrior poses while giving our minds something specific to think about: Gratitude.

Begin in your Mountain Pose and take a moment to pause here. Remember that Mountain Pose is much more than simply standing. Be mindful about feeling your feet connect with the floor, your spine growing tall, your arms reaching down, and your belly becoming engaged.

1 **Set yourself up for Warrior One**
Step your right foot back at a 45-degree angle.
Hips are square to the front of the room.
Bend into your front knee.
Reach your arms up alongside your ears.
Soften your shoulders.
In your Warrior One, think of one thing that you are grateful for.

2 **Move into Warrior Two**
Straighten your front leg.
Turn your back foot out to a 90-degree angle.
Bend back into your front knee.
Bring your arms into a T-position.
Look over your front center finger.
In your Warrior Two, think of another thing you are grateful for.

3 **Peaceful Warrior**
Flip your front palm to the sky.
Keep your eyes on your front hand and reach it up and back.
Allow your back hand to rest gently on your back leg.
In your Peaceful Warrior, think of one more thing you are grateful for.
Now come back to your Warrior Two and remember the second thing you thought of. Come back to Warrior One and recall the first thing you thought of. Without making a sound, return to Mountain Pose. Let's try this on the other side, but this time we'll make it a little bit more challenging.

4 **Set yourself up for Warrior One**
Step your right foot back at a 45-degree angle.
Hips are square to the front of the room.
Bend into your front knee.
Reach your arms up alongside your ears.
Soften your shoulders.
In your Warrior One, think of one person that you are grateful for.

5 **Move into Warrior Two**
Straighten your front leg.
Turn your back foot out to a 90-degree angle.
Bend back into your front knee.
Bring your arms into a T-position.
Look over your front center finger.
In your Warrior Two, think of one place you are grateful for.

6 **Peaceful Warrior**
Flip your front palm to the sky.
Keep your eyes on your front hand and reach it up and back.
Allow your back hand to rest gently on your back leg.
In your Peaceful Warrior, think of a day in your life you are grateful to have experienced.
Now come back to Warrior Two and remember the place you thought of. Come back to Warrior One and recall the person you thought of. Return to Mountain Pose and smile.

Day Gratitude Yoga Nap

Today we will practice our gratitude in a Yoga Nap. Begin by coming into your Yoga Nap space and pose. Remember to unravel your body as much as possible in order to let yourself completely relax.

With your arms by your side or on your belly, begin to melt away any tension you are holding onto. Take a long, slow, deep breath in, and just as it came in, let your breath go slowly out. Feel any stress melt away with each breath you take.

Breathe in, breathe out.
Breathe in, breathe out.
Breathe in, breathe out.

Let yourself be fully here, right now. There is nothing you need to do at this moment except relax.

With your eyes closed, use your imagination to picture a person that you are thankful for. Maybe you can even imagine a picture of them smiling. Think the words, "Thank you for being you," in your mind as you feel how grateful you are for all the good things they bring to your life.

Pause for twenty seconds.

Now imagine in your mind a place that you are very thankful for. Imagine every detail that you can recall about that place; what it looks like, what it smells like. Think about if there are other people there, or if you are alone. Imagine what it feels like to be there, and think the words, "Thank you for being there."

Pause for thirty seconds.

Begin to bring to mind an object that you are thankful for. Maybe it is something you take for granted, like warm socks on a cold day or the sunshine on your face in the summer. Maybe it is something that is very valuable and special to you. Maybe you have a few things that want to come to your mind right now, and that is okay too! Think the words, "Thank you for these items and what they bring to my life."

Pause for thirty seconds.

Bring to your mind your favorite food. Remember the last time you got to eat that food; how it tasted, and who you were with. Think the words, "Thank you for the food that nourishes me."

Pause for thirty seconds.

Now think about something that your body allows you to do that you are thankful for. Maybe it is a sport you play, writing you have done, or a creative skill you have. Maybe it is the ability to fish, play an instrument, or hug a family member. Take a moment to say, "Thank you," to your body for allowing you to do the things you love.

Pause for thirty seconds.

If there is anything else that comes to mind right now that you would like to express gratitude for, simply think the words, "Thank you," over and over again.

Pause for thirty seconds.

As we exit our Yoga Nap, slowly begin to deepen your inhales and exhales. Keep this feeling of gratitude with you as you begin to wiggle your fingers and toes and give yourself any gentle stretch that feels good. Slowly roll onto one side, and then gently make your way to a seated position.

Day **Responding to a Worry**

This practice is called Responding to a Worry. It gives you the opportunity to write down something that has been bothering you, and to receive anonymous advice about it from a peer. Just like we wrote out and ripped up our fears or concerns in the Getting Rid of Your Worries practice, this exercise helps you to get something off of your mind.

To do this exercise, you will write down something negative that has been on your mind. Maybe it is a stressor, like a big test coming up, or maybe it is the concern of an unknown, like not knowing which classes you will take next year. Maybe it is something that is bothering you, such as your best friend not inviting you to do something with them.

You will not write your name on the paper, so nobody will know this concern is coming from you. Please remember that someone else is going to read this, so it should be something you are comfortable with someone else hearing. It should also not include too many personal details.

Once you have written down your worry, you will rip out your piece of paper, crumple it up, and toss it toward *(assign a designated spot in the room)*. Next, we will all get up, choose a piece of paper, and take it back to our seats to read. Once you have read this person's worry, you will either write a piece of advice, a positive affirmation, or words of encouragement on the page.

Remember to do this with sincerity: This is someone's real worry or concern, and it deserves to be taken seriously. Once you have written a response, you will crumple the paper back up and gently toss it to *(the designated spot)*. We will repeat this two more times: Selecting a worry, reading it, writing a response, crumpling it back up, and tossing it back. When we are finished, I will ask for a few volunteers to read a worry and the responses on the paper out loud to the class.

TEACHER DIRECTIONS:
- *Instruct students to write down their worries.*
- *Students tear these papers out of their journals.*
- *When all students are finished, crumple up the papers and toss them toward the designated spot in the room.*
- *Students all get a piece of paper, read the worry, and write a response to it.*
- *When all are done writing a response, crumple papers back up and toss them back to the designated spot.*
- *Repeat this two more times, but be sure to wait until everyone is finished writing their responses so they are all tossing papers at the same time.*
- *After as many rounds as you would like, ask for at least three volunteers to read the worries and the responses on the paper they are holding.*

Day 4-7-8 Breath

Today we will do a seated breathing practice to help calm our nervous systems. Your nervous system has two responses: Rest and Relaxation; and Fight, Flight, or Freeze. This breath practice helps you to activate the Rest and Relaxation system in your body. It also helps to reduce anxiety, and can even help you to sleep.

To do this practice, begin in your seated posture with your feet against the earth. Push your back into the chair and keep a proud, tall spine. See what muscles you can relax here.

Begin by closing your eyes and noticing your natural breath. In this 4-7-8 Breath, we will inhale for four seconds, hold the breath for seven seconds, and exhale for eight seconds.

It is natural for the mind to experience a bit of concern when holding the breath for extended periods of time. If this feels uncomfortable for you to practice, please allow your breath to move as it best serves you and your body.

Breathe in 1-2-3-4
Hold 1-2-3-4-5-6-7
Breathe out 1-2-3-4-5-6-7-8

Repeat 5-10 times.

Allow your breath to return to normal. Remember that you can do this practice any time you would like. All you need to do is find a quiet space and count your breaths. When you are ready, open your eyes.

Day 40   Gratitude Alphabet

This activity involves the use of paper/journal and a writing utensil.
Instruct students to rip a piece of paper out of their notebooks.

There are countless things to be grateful for! We can practice showing gratitude in a variety of ways such as sending thank you notes, telling someone we appreciate them, building a Gratitude Jar, or making a gratitude list. Today you are going to make a gratitude list, and I challenge you to make a list using each letter of the alphabet in order to complete the ABC's of gratitude.

Please write the letters of the alphabet on the far left side of your paper, allowing one line per letter. Next, go through and write down something you are grateful for that starts with each letter. You may choose to write one word or a complete sentence on each line. After you are finished, we will go through the alphabet sharing our responses for each letter.

Give students time to write their gratitude alphabet, and make one for yourself too! When your students are finished, have your students share, making sure to get at least one response per letter of the alphabet.

Day Just Listen

Today's practice asks you to use the skill of listening. Oftentimes during a conversation, we are just waiting for our turn to talk and are not truly listening to everything being said to us.

Sometimes we have a hard time listening because we have so many things going on in our minds that we can't focus on what is being said to us. Other times, we are distracted by the noises happening around us.

In this activity, you will close your eyes and see if you can identify any sounds in the classroom that you normally do not notice. Begin in your posture for a seated practice. Take a deep breath in, then let it go completely. Breathe in, and out. Breathe in, and out.

As you become quiet in your body and your mind, maybe you can begin to hear the sound of your breath as it goes quietly in and out.

Pause for ten seconds.

What other noises can you identify? Maybe the ticking of a clock.

Pause for ten seconds.

Maybe you can hear sounds in the hallway.

Pause for ten seconds.

Maybe you can hear noises outside.

Pause for ten seconds.

Maybe you can even notice the space between the sounds - silence itself has a sound.

Pause for thirty seconds.

Notice all of the sounds that exist around you, then begin to come back to the sound of your own breath as you breathe in...and out. Breathe in...and out. Breathe in...and out.

Remember to pause often and take in everything happening around you without worry or judgement. When you are ready, open your eyes.

Day Remembering Your Inner Best Friend

This activity involves the use of paper/journal and a writing utensil.
Instruct students to take out their papers and writing utensils.

If someone else talked about you the way you think about or talk about yourself, would you choose to be friends with them? Think about this seriously. How often do you jokingly, or not jokingly, put yourself down by saying things like, "I am so stupid," or, "I look horrible today." The chances are that if you have spoken about yourself like that out loud, you have unconsciously had that thought multiple times in your mind. It is time for us to be kinder to ourselves.

A few weeks ago, you analyzed things your Inner Best Friend might say to you versus what your Inner Critic says. Remember: Your Inner Best Friend is just like your real best friend. It is the voice that tells you even though you made a mistake and forgot your homework, you are still a smart and capable person. Conversely, your Inner Critic is the voice that criticizes what you do and tells you that you are not good enough.

We all have an Inner Critic and an Inner Best Friend, and each of us gets to decide who gets the microphone in our mind. Maybe now that we have been practicing Mindfulness, you are able to hear the two different voices more clearly in your mind. Turn to a fresh page in your journal and write down what you have been hearing your Inner Best Friend and your Inner Critic say to you lately. Notice if anything has changed.

Possible prompts for small or large group sharing after journal reflection:
What is some of your negative self-talk?
How can you change those statements into more positive self-talk?
What is something positive you can practice saying to yourself each day, either in your mind or out loud?

Day The Power of Positive Thinking

*This **activity can include** the use of laptops, tablets, smartphones, or a trip to your library. You may choose to either read these benefits from the Mayo Clinic to your class, or you can put them in partners/small groups and ask them to find credible resources that offer the benefits of positive thinking.*

Much like gratitude, positive thinking offers a lot of benefits that have very little to do with thinking itself. With partners, please spend five minutes researching the benefits of positive thinking. We will compile a list when you are finished.

Health benefits of positive thinking:
- Longer life expectancy
- Decreased anxiety and stress
- Stronger immune system
- More positive mood
- Better physical and emotional well-being
- Better cardiovascular health
- Stronger coping skills during stressful times

Our thinking is important; whether it is our thinking about ourselves, others, or a life circumstance. We can use Mindfulness to help train our brains to think more positively, and we can also use positive thinking and messages to help inspire others.

Tomorrow's activity invites you to have students leave positive Post-it Notes anonymously on lockers for students. If you choose to follow this activity as outlined, please send a quick email to your building principal and custodian letting them know the intention behind this activity and asking if they would like for you to modify it.

This activity requires a large number of pens and Post-it Notes. You may choose to adapt this activity in any way you wish to accommodate your students and your school policies. The intention is that students leave anonymous positive messages for others to find on their lockers.

If you are completing this workbook with one classroom section, you will want to give students enough Post-its to fill the lockers, or come close to it.

Possible adaptations: Students leaving Post-its only for their peers in class, students writing Post-its for teachers in your building, students leaving digital messages for others, or filling a bulletin board with positive messages. Regardless of the scale, be cognizant of who is receiving multiple messages, and who is receiving only a few or none at all. For example, if you are having students write for staff, help ensure that one staff does not receive five messages while others get zero.

Today, we are going to take our positivity outside of the classroom and into our school. In a few moments, I am going to give each of you *(number of)* Post-it Notes. Your mission is to write positive messages on these and leave them anonymously on lockers in the school.

It is important your message is something that almost anyone can relate to, and that it is something that makes people smile when they see it. You are welcome to research positive quotes on the Internet, write a positive affirmation, or offer a piece of advice for someone. You are also welcome to doodle on or decorate these however you wish. I will approve all Post-it Notes before they are passed out.

We will keep this activity anonymous, meaning do not tell anyone it was you or your class that wrote these messages. This activity is meant to be seen as an intentional act of kindness. This activity asks you to share some positivity with others!

Pass out five Post-it Notes to each student. Be sure to monitor student work. Ask to see and approve all messages before they are passed out. Consider having all students go to the hall at once under your supervision, or assign two to three students at a time to leave the room to stick them on lockers.

Day Positive Post-It for Yourself

This activity requires the use of one Post-it Note, index card,
or small piece of paper per student.

Yesterday, we offered positive messages for others. It is wonderful to share positivity with others and know you made someone's day a little bit brighter. Maybe you were even able to see people's reactions when they saw the positive Post-its!

Just as it is important to be kind to others, we need to practice this same kindness for ourselves. Today, you will write yourself a positive message that you want to see every day. This Post-it can be displayed anywhere you know you will see it every day. Perhaps you can place it somewhere like your locker, in your car, on your bathroom mirror, or on your refrigerator.

Please be thoughtful when writing your message to yourself, just like you were for others. Remember, you can write an inspirational quote you find online, a positive affirmation, words of encouragement, or a reminder to smile.

Give your students time to create their positive Post-its. Monitor that they are offering themselves positive messages. Perhaps provide the opportunity for students to share their messages with the whole class or a partner.

Day 46   Revisiting Mantra Breathing

Today we will revisit mantra, or positive affirmation, breathing. In this type of breathing, we help to focus the mind by offering ourselves mantras to the count of three on each inhale, and repeat the same with each exhale. For example, inhale I-Am-Happy, exhale I-Am-Happy *(to slow count of three)*.

As you know, we can sometimes be negative to ourselves and put ourselves down. Mantra Breathing helps us to be more compassionate and positive in our own minds. It helps to train the mind to be our Inner Best Friend even more.

Today I will be guiding you through Mantra Breathing, but I will be leaving you more space to guide yourself in the practice. Remember, this activity will also help you focus, so continue to return your mind back to your slow three count affirmation on each inhale and each exhale.

Find your comfortable seated position with your tall spine and your feet pressing against the floor. Begin to close your eyes or take your gaze to the ground. Let's start with counting breaths:

Inhale 1-2-3, Exhale 3-2-1
Inhale 1-2-3, Exhale 3-2-1

Now let's replace the numbers with affirmations:

Inhale I-Am-Happy, Exhale I-Am-Happy
Inhale I-Am-Capable, Exhale I-Am-Capable
Inhale I-Am-Enough, Exhale I-Am-Enough

For the next two minutes, repeat this affirmation breathing using your own positive affirmation at the end.

After one minute, you might choose to say, "If you notice your mind has wandered, gently bring it back to your Mantra Breathing."

Take a deep breath in,
Take a deep breath out,
And open your eyes.

Allow for whole class or small group discussion about whether it was easy or challenging for them to focus their minds today.

Day 47 Positive Affirmation Circle

Bring students to sit in a circle or turn desks to all face one another.

We have worked a lot with positive affirmations in order to help build up our Inner Best Friends. Remember, a positive affirmation is something you say you are, or something you want to become. It begins with "I Am", and ends with something positive. It is called a positive affirmation because it affirms, or says something is true.

However, it is not enough that we say this to ourselves. We should also surround ourselves with people who affirm positive things about us. For today's activity, you will choose one positive affirmation for yourself to share with the class, such as "I Am Creative", "I Am Athletic", or "I Am Loving". After you say your positive affirmation out loud, the class will respond with the words, "Yes you are!" to strengthen your belief that you are!

Have students go around the circle sharing their positive affirmations. After each person shares, the class will respond with, "Yes you are!" Be sure you share one too!

Day 48 Brainstorming Intentional Acts of Kindness

We often hear about random acts of kindness. A random act of kindness is when someone does something nice out of the blue for someone else. While this act might be random to the person who receives it, the action is completely intentional, or on purpose, by the person who did it. The Positive Post-It Project was a great example of a random act of kindness that was done intentionally by us. Today, we are going to brainstorm other intentional acts of kindness we can do as individuals or as a class. We will complete these acts of kindness on Day Fifty. During your brainstorm, these are some things to keep in mind:

• an act of kindness can impact only one person and still be beneficial.
• each act needs to be completed in 5-10 minutes.
• all acts must not require any kind of cost.
• each act must positively impact the receiver.

For this activity, determine if you would like for the students to brainstorm in partners or as a class. Decide if you would like for students to complete these acts of kindness individually, with partners, or if this will be a whole class activity based on the types of ideas. Students may use the Internet to help guide their search. Tomorrow's Mindfulness exercise is dedicated to planning for completion of these projects.

Day Planning Intentional Acts of Kindness

Use this day to plan or organize anything needed for completing Intentional Acts of Kindness. If this day is not necessary for you, please revisit Day Six, Triangle Breathing.

Day Intentional Acts of Kindness

As a class, or individually, students complete their intentional acts of kindness.

Day Stress Management

This activity involves the use of paper/journal and a writing utensil. Instruct students to take out their papers and writing utensils.

Today we are going to talk about stress. To put it simply, stress is a normal reaction your body has when change occurs. You can experience stress physically, mentally, and emotionally. Sometimes you feel stress in all three ways. What are some things in your life that cause you stress?

Take a few responses. If your students are struggling to come up with answers, offer a few suggestions like the pressure of figuring out what to do after high school, managing a full schedule, or relationship issues with family/friends/significant others.

Stress is something that everyone experiences to various degrees in their lives. It does not matter what you look like, how much money you make, or where you live - every single person experiences different types of stressors. As you get older, the types of stressors you experience change. Maybe you can see that your stressors now are much different than they were when you were twelve.

It is important to manage stress because, if left unresolved, it can negatively impact your physical health, emotional well-being, and mental stability. Over the next few days, we will explore positive stress management techniques. Before we do, however, let's hear ones that you already use. Please write a few stress management techniques you know and practice in your journals.

Allow students time to write their stress management strategies and then share a few as a whole class.

Today I am going to show you a few yoga poses for stress management. These poses are effective in helping to relieve stress because we hold muscle tension when we experience stress. These poses help to release the tension from the muscles. By helping the body to relax, we also help the mind to relax. In these poses it is especially important to remember to take deep breaths. You are welcome to use the counting breathing that you know to help even out your inhales and exhales.

CHILD'S POSE

Come onto your hands and knees. Bring your knees wide and your big toes together to touch. Allow your hips to sink back toward your heels, and extend your arms long out in front of you. Let your forehead come toward the earth. If you would like, you can walk your hands over to the left, stretching through your side body, and then over to the right. *Guide students through three inhales and exhales here.*

SEATED FORWARD FOLD

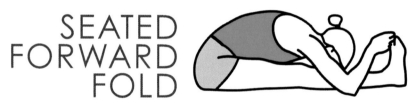

Extend your legs out in front of you, and flex your toes back toward your nose. If you notice that your hamstrings in the back of your legs are very tight, you may choose to have a slight or deep bend in the knees. Sit up with a tall spine, just like you do when getting yourself ready for seated practice. Align your belly button, heart, chin, and crown of your head. Inhale; reach your arms up over your head and pause. As you exhale, imagine reaching up and over a beach ball on your legs, and begin to fold forward. Allow your hands to rest gently where they fall; maybe on the thighs, shins, or the feet. This pose only helps with stress management when we are not forcing anything. If you notice you are pulling yourself to get deeper into the stretch, see where you can relax. Soften your head and look down to enjoy the full benefits of this pose. *Guide students through three inhales and exhales here.*

BUTTERFLY POSE

Sitting up tall and proud, bend your knees and bring the soles of the feet together to touch. Place your hands on the front of your shins, your feet, or put them on the earth behind you to help you sit up taller. Pause here for a deep inhale and exhale. Feel your shoulders relax down your back. Soften the muscles of your face, and allow the knees to work their way toward the earth, recognizing that it might be a long journey to get there. If you would like to, you can stay seated tall; or you have the option to hinge from your hips, and gently fold forward. Remember the goal in all of these poses is to help release tension, not create it. Do not worry about how far down your knees go, or how far forward you fold. Instead, focus on how much you can relax. *Guide students through three inhales and exhales here.*

STANDING SIDE STRETCH

Begin in Mountain Pose with your feet underneath your hips. Keep your legs slightly active with a tall spine and your tailbone reaching toward the ground. Relax your shoulders and keep your arms by your sides. Inhale; reach both arms up overhead and grab hold of your right wrist with your left hand. Inhale to lengthen through the spine, exhale to send your hips to the right and reach the arms to the left. Inhale and come back to center. Switch the grip of your hands to let the right hand take hold of the left wrist. Inhale to reach and grow tall; as you exhale send your hips to the left and arms to the right. *Repeat this twice more on both sides.*

Day Proactive vs Reactive Stress Management

This activity involves the use of paper/journal and a writing utensil.
Instruct students to take out their papers and writing utensils.

We know that stress impacts us physically, mentally, and emotionally. Therefore, it is important that we have stress management techniques to use when we feel stressed. However, it is also very important that we have stress management techniques to use before we ever feel stressed to maintain a healthy mind during daily life. This is called Proactive Stress Management versus Reactive Stress Management.

Proactive Stress Management includes the things you do on a daily and weekly basis for your overall self-care. These could include exercise, making a To-Do list each week, getting enough sleep, knowing when you need to take a break, or keeping a positive mental attitude.

Proactive Stress Management helps to keep us on track before we experience any type of stress. Think about it like this: If you see a movie with a group of friends on Friday, and on Saturday you all receive a message that one of your friends has come down with a cold, you might not catch it if you have already been taking vitamins, getting enough rest, working out, and eating healthy foods in your daily life. Hopefully with all of these preventative measures, your immune system will be strong enough to fight off the cold.

On the other hand, another friend could easily get the same cold you were exposed to if they haven't been maintaining a healthy life-style by running on little sleep, eating mostly fast food, and generally neglecting to take care of their body and mind.

Stress works the same way. If we are proactive about taking care of our bodies and minds, we are less likely to be completely derailed when stress comes our way.

Reactive Stress Management is what you do when you notice you are already stressed and you need help calming down. There are a lot of healthy options for Reactive Stress Management, such as taking five deep breaths, taking a Yoga Nap, getting outside, journaling, talking with a friend or parent, or exercising. Healthy Reactive Stress Management techniques help us to deal with the stress head-on rather than avoiding the stress with unhealthy strategies like binge watching Netflix or procrastinating.

We need to be mindful of how we respond when we are stressed so we are not creating more pressure for ourselves down the line. Taking a break is very beneficial, but we need to be sure we are not simply avoiding the stressors because that actually ends up creating more stress in the long run.

Please take out your journals and make a list of Proactive Stress Management techniques you already practice or would like to practice. Then, do the same for healthy Reactive Stress Management techniques. And finally, list any avoidant coping strategies you have used in the past to not deal with your stress.

Opportunity for whole class share out or partner discussions.

Day Progressive Muscle Relaxation

Another way we can manage stress proactively or reactively is by taking a Yoga Nap. Set yourself up now for your Yoga Nap. Find a comfortable position lying down on your back with your arms by your side. Know that you are completely safe here; know that you can relax here.

Today's Mindfulness practice is a Progressive Body Scan, and its goal is to totally relax our bodies so that our minds and our emotions can relax too.

In this exercise you will bring your attention to one body part, tense the muscles in that area, and then relax them completely. Be kind to your body and try not to strain while doing this. The goal is to help you ease any tension you have been holding onto. It is important to keep breathing throughout this exercise.

Begin by taking a full breath in, and a full breath out. Breathe in deeply, and breathe out completely.
Breathe in and out.
Bring your attention to your feet.
Take a deep breath in and curl your toes and tense your feet.

Pause for a few seconds.

Exhale and relax all of the muscles of your feet.
Notice how your feet feel more relaxed than they did a moment ago.

Pause for a few seconds.

Inhale and gently tighten the muscles of your lower legs.

Pause for a few seconds.

Exhale and relax your legs completely.

Pause for a few seconds.

Think about the muscles in your upper thighs.
Inhale and squeeze the muscles of the upper thighs. Hold your knees together like you are squeezing a penny between them.

Pause for a few seconds.

Exhale and relax the whole lower portion of your body.
Gently begin arching your lower back on your inhale.

Pause for a few seconds.

Exhale completely and relax your lower back into the earth.
Inhale, feel your belly rise and fill with air and pause. Feel your belly full of air.
Exhale and let your belly be soft and completely relaxed.

Pause for a few seconds.

Repeat this same feeling in your chest. Take a deep breath in, feeling your belly and chest fill with air, and pause. Exhale completely let it go, noticing how the breath can move easier in your body now.

Pause for a few seconds.

Inhale and pull your shoulders up toward your ears like you are shrugging.

Pause for a few seconds.

Exhale and relax your shoulders as far away from your head as you can.

Pause for a few seconds.

Inhale and tighten all of the muscles in your arms; make fists with your hands.

Pause for a few seconds.

Exhale and let your arms and hands soften. Notice how your palms are more open as they face up to the sky.
Let go of all stress as you breathe in.
See where else you can relax as you breathe out.
Inhale, begin to tighten the muscles of your face by scrunching your whole face together.

Pause for a few seconds.

Exhale to relax all the muscles of your face, noticing how all of the wrinkles are taken out of your forehead.

Pause for a few seconds.

Notice for a moment how it feels to have a relaxed body.
Maybe you notice a few areas that still feel tight or tense.
To help those areas relax even more, inhale gently and squeeze all of the muscles in your body tight like a ball, then exhale and let everything melt back into the ground.
One more inhale and tighten like a ball; exhale and relax deeper.

Pause for thirty seconds.

This feeling of being relaxed is always available to you.
All you need to do is connect to your breathing and ask parts of your body to relax.
When we do this, we let our minds slow down, our bodies unwind, and our emotions calm down.
With this relaxed state, take a deep breath in; let it go completely.
Do this three more times on your own.

Pause for thirty seconds.

Slowly begin to wiggle your fingers and toes, bringing small movements back to your body.
On your next inhale take whatever stretch feels good for you.
And slowly, quietly, find your way back to a seated position.

Day Stress Inventory

This activity involves the use of paper/journal and a writing utensil.
Instruct students to take out their papers and writing utensils.

Stress shows up for all of us in different ways. Sometimes we do not pick up on the subtle cues that we are stressed until we are almost to the point of a full meltdown. Today you will think about some of the signs your body gives you when you are experiencing stress by responding to the following questions in your journal:

1. Where do I physically feel stress in my body?
   EXAMPLES
   clenched jaw, grinding teeth while sleeping, tight shoulders, stomach ache

2. What are my thoughts like when I am stressed?
   EXAMPLES
   racing thoughts, Inner Critic tells me I am not doing enough

3. What do I notice happens to my emotions when I am stressed?
   EXAMPLES
   shutting down and not talking to anyone, crying, feeling overwhelmed, feeling agitated

4. The next time I notice I am experiencing any of these things I can:
   Make a list of positive stress management techniques.
   EXAMPLES
   take a walk, talk with a friend, parent, or coach, practice a yoga nap, do deep breathing, make a to-do list, give myself positive affirmations

Opportunity for whole class share or partner discussions.

Stress Inventory - - - - - - - - ->

Use arrows to show where you feel stress in your body.

EXAMPLES:
- tight shoulders
- scrunched face
- clenched fists
- sweaty palms

Day Old Habits

Remain a little bit mysterious for this activity.

In today's Mindfulness practice, we will begin with an activity and end with a discussion.

Can I please have five volunteers come to the front of the room?
Once they get there, instruct them to walk back to their seats.

Most of us would walk to the front of the room just like they did. Sometimes we do things on autopilot. You are now invited to use your creativity.

With a partner, please brainstorm five completely different ways that you could come to the front of the room.

EXAMPLES: crawling, piggy back rides, walking backwards, hopping

Give students time to come up with ways they could move to the front of the room. Ask for five new volunteers to show their alternative ways to come up to the front of the room.

DISCUSSION
You may lead this with your students however you see fit, or simply read this aloud.

We are creatures of habit. Sometimes we do things without even thinking about them because it is what we have always done. Most people would not even think about coming to the front of the classroom any other way than walking because it is normal and socially acceptable.

While it is not appropriate for you to jump up to the front of the classroom in any given scenario, there are times in life that we need to look at our old ways of doing things, and see if there is another way we can accomplish that same task that might be more fun, easier, or more beneficial.

Old patterns can easily become entrenched in the mind, develop as habits, and eventually become our daily patterns. Sometimes we need to change negative patterns of behavior or simply change the way we do things in order to keep ourselves challenged and excited.

Take a moment to allow the class to brainstorm different morning routines or after school routines.

Day Mindful Attention

You will want to identify an item in the room that you want your students to describe/recall. Please consider choosing one that is unique to your classroom and has memorable details.

Mindfulness happens when we are paying attention to our experiences; what is happening around us and within us. We may think we are paying close attention to our surroundings or a task at hand, only to realize we are actually distracted by the thoughts in our heads or activities around us.

For this activity, we will rely on mindful memories. Begin by finding your seated posture, sitting with a tall spine. Please close your eyes or take your eyes to your lap. Take a nice long inhale, and feel your shoulders relax as you exhale. Repeat this two more times, softening anywhere you might be holding onto stress.

In your mind, picture everything that you can about this classroom. Think about where things are placed, where people sit; maybe you can even think of details like what was written on the board or hanging on the wall. Now, think of *(your chosen object)*:

• Can you picture where it is placed in the room? Recall every detail about this that you can in your mind.

• Offer some cues specific to your item. If appropriate, ask about texture, colors,
   details. Do your best to recreate this item in your mind.

Pause for one to two minutes.

In a moment, you will silently open your eyes and bring your attention to *(your chosen object)*. When you do so, allow the details of this item to come to you. Maybe you see things you did not remember before. Maybe you realize you did a great job of recalling everything about it.

Mindfulness can improve the quality of our lives by asking us to slow down and notice the little details of our surroundings; whether that is a person, a place, or an experience. I invite you to try this activity at home today.

Day   Peaceful Stream • By Anne Funke

Another way Mindfulness adds to our quality of life is by reducing our stress levels. One of the best ways to reduce stress is through guided imagery or a Yoga Nap. Today's practice offers a Yoga Nap combined with a story that asks you to use your imagination. Do your best to envision all of the story in your mind to help you relax more fully.

Close your eyes and find a comfortable position lying down. Place your arms at your side for a moment and take deep breaths in and out of your nose. Feel your body relax onto the floor. Allow yourself to feel comfortable, safe, at peace. As you breathe here, feel your mind and your body release any worry, anxiety, or tension you might be feeling. You are peaceful, and you are calm.

Pause for a few seconds.

As you continue to breathe, start to imagine the color blue in your mind. This blue might be light, or it might be dark. You might see the color vividly, or maybe the color blue has a shape in your mind. The color blue is calming, peaceful, relaxing. Imagine your blue for a couple more breaths.

Pause for a few seconds.

Now imagine that you wade into a shallow stream and begin to journey down it, the water as blue as the sky. Maybe you're floating in a canoe, or a tube, a raft, or perhaps you are swimming with nothing at all. As you make your way into the stream's slow current, you feel weightless, free, and peaceful. The warm sun is gently shining on your skin.

The water is safe and calm. You are safe and calm. There is no rush to be anywhere. There is no rush to do anything. You are floating down the stream, enjoying the peaceful present moment. You have no worries. You feel still, calm and at peace, and as we gently breathe in and exhale out, we are increasing this sense of calm.

What else do you notice about your surroundings? Are there birds softly chirping? Can you hear the water lapping against the rocks? Are there trees by the stream swaying gently in the breeze? What do the clouds look like in the sky? Everything around you adds to your sense of calm and peace. There is no rush, there are no distractions. You are perfectly present to all your surroundings.

All is well. All is good. Everything is as it should be. You are in exactly the right place.

You realize the stream is starting to come to an end, and you savor the last few moments before stepping onto the shore once again. You picture the cool blue water, the sun shining down, the sounds of the water hitting the rocks, and memorize this feeling of peace and calm and presence. You know you can imagine yourself in this place any time you feel worried, or stressed, or upset. You can remember this place in order to feel peaceful and still.

Start to move your body gently by wiggling your fingers and toes. Let your head fall from side to side. Move with a sense of ease and lightness. You are not rushed, you are calm. Take your arms above your head, feeling light, and take a full body stretch. Hug your knees in and roll over to the right side of your body. Rest here for a moment and feel a sense of gratitude for all your body does for you.

Day Notice Your "Stories"

Mindfulness helps us to watch our thoughts in a really powerful way. Sometimes our minds create "stories" about situations that stress us out more than the actual situation itself. It is important to notice these "stories" because they are often created by the Inner Critic.

For example, say you have a science test coming up and you are absolutely worked up over it. Ask yourself to pause and notice what you are worried about. Maybe you are not actually stressed out about the science test itself. Maybe you are actually stressed out about the story you have created around the science test.

When you notice yourself feeling stressed or anxious, ask yourself:

" What is the story here? "

The story might be:

" I am going to fail this test. "

When you notice the story you are telling yourself, you can look at what is happening more objectively. If you want to do well on the test, you know the next steps to take involve studying and asking for assistance when needed. Get rid of the story in your mind and look at what is actually happening.

"Stories" happen a lot in social situations. We might find we are stressed about a friend asking us to do something that we do not actually want to do. In reality, we are not usually stressed about the decision itself. What we are stressed about is the story we have created around what we assume people might think or say about us. For example, we might think, "If I do not do this, then nobody will like me." This story is untrue. SOME people might not like the decision you made, but that does not mean that nobody will like you.

When you notice that you are feeling worked up, look for the stories that are playing in your mind and ask if it is your Inner Best Friend or your Inner Critic that created the story. Your thoughts are NOT facts. Look for the facts of the situation to help slow your stories down.

Day   Moving Beyond the Story

Sometimes the negative stories we create in our brains stop us from accomplishing things that are within our potential. If we tell ourselves we will never be able to do something, we are often afraid to even try doing it because of the story in our mind--even if we practice that skill and have the capabilities.

We are going to practice a yoga pose today, and while we do, I want you to notice if you begin to tell yourself a story in your mind about never being able to do it. In yoga, flexibility and strength start in the mind and then transfer to being able to do it in the body. What that means is you must be open to all possibilities and believe that you can do anything you put your mind to.

STANDING FORWARD FOLD
Begin in Mountain Pose with your feet underneath your hips, a soft bend in your knees, and your arms by your side. As you inhale, reach your arms up overhead. As you exhale, put a deep bend in your knees and fold forward over your legs. Allow your head and neck to relax completely here.

The bend in your knees helps to protect your lower back and allows for a gentle stretch through the backs of the legs. Take a deep breath in and let it go. Notice the story that is playing right now in your mind. Can you listen to it without letting it take over? Maybe you notice it comment on your f lexibility, or lack thereof. Can you look for the facts? If you stretch often, if you breathe deep, your muscles will eventually relax and your legs will become straighter. Slowly feel your feet push into the earth below you, and roll up your spine to come to standing.

HAND TO TOE/KNEE
Find your Mountain Pose; tall, strong, stable, silent. Begin to transfer your weight into your left foot. Gently use your core muscles to pull your right knee up into the chest. Reach your right hand for the front of your right shin. Stand up even taller here to avoid the natural tendency to hunch your shoulders forward.

You can stay here, or you can see if you can grab your right foot with your right hand to extend the leg forward. You can stay here, or you can switch your left hand onto your right knee or foot and slowly twist open to the right, looking over your right shoulder. Breathe.

Wherever you are, inhale fully and exhale completely. Notice if you have a story in your mind. Notice if you are comparing yourself to other people in the room. Look for the facts. Listen to your Inner Best Friend. Take one more full breath in, and let it go completely to come back to your Mountain Pose.

Repeat on the other side.

Day **61** Anchor Breathing

Anchor Breathing is a type of breath that helps keep us grounded in the present moment. Just as an anchor holds a ship in place, this breath practice helps to still our bodies and minds to be present to the here and now.

In this practice we will focus on the breath with four options for hand placements on the body. The option that feels best for you will depend on where you feel your breath most strongly. There is no right or wrong answer, just what feels good for you.

Demonstrate each hand placement while explaining orally.

You will have the option to:
- keep your hands in your lap and simply notice the breath in each of these places
- place both hands on your belly
- place one hand on your belly and one on your heart
- place one hand underneath your nose. Palm facing down, fingers together, index finger against the space between the nose and mouth.

Begin in your seated posture. Sit with a tall spine, roll your shoulders away from your ears, and reach the crown of your head up toward the sky. Close your eyes or take your gaze down to your lap or the floor. Allow your hands to rest gently in your lap and begin to notice your breathing. Notice that when you inhale your belly and chest rise, and as you exhale, they fall.

Pause for a few seconds.

Notice how your torso also expands laterally, allowing your side body to get bigger on the inhale and smaller on the exhale.

Pause for a few seconds.

Feel the cool air as it enters your nostrils; notice the warm air as it leaves your nostrils.

Pause for a few seconds.

You are welcome to keep your hands in your lap if that feels most comfortable for you, but I invite you to try these hand placements to further your connection with your body and breath. Place both hands on your belly. You may choose to have them on your side body or on the front of your belly. See if you can bring all of your attention to the breath moving in and out of the belly.

Pause for a few seconds.

Keep one hand on your belly and take the other to your heart. Recognize the breath flowing freely through the belly and chest on your inhales and exhales.

Pause for a few seconds.

Finally, relax one hand in your lap and take the other beneath your nose. Feel the cool air travel across your fingers when you breathe in. Feel the warm air travel across your fingers as you breathe out.

Pause for a few seconds.

Take a moment to recognize which anchor helped you to connect with your breath most fully. We will take five breaths together. Find the hand placement that felt the best for you.

Inhale, Exhale.
Inhale, Exhale.
Inhale, Exhale.
Inhale, Exhale.
Inhale, Exhale.

Know that this anchor is available to you at any time you want to feel grounded, connected, or present. When you are ready, release your arms and open your eyes.

Day

Noticing Wandering Thoughts

This activity involves the use of a timer and a bell. You may choose to set an alarm to go off on your phone at the set time intervals, or keep track of time yourself and ring a bell or offer another soft sound of your choice.

Being mindful helps us to become more aware of our thoughts, body, and emotions. Today, we will notice how our thoughts can wander off during a meditation. Remember, it is normal for your mind to think - that is its job after all. With practice, however, we can train the mind to become more focused and more positive, which allows us to use our mind more fully to our advantage.

We will begin in your seated posture and focus our attention on the breath.This exercise invites you to come back to the present moment by utilizing the sound of the bell. Every so often you will hear this sound *(play sound of your choice)* and when you do, that is your invitation to return your attention to your breath if your mind has wandered. This is a great way to become more aware of how our thoughts can wander, and to learn how to bring our minds back to the present moment without judgement of ourselves.

Begin in your seated posture with a tall spine and your feet rooted into the earth.
When you are ready, close your eyes.
Take a deep breath in, and exhale your breath out completely.
We will do this three more times together.
Breathe in fully, then exhale and relax into this moment completely.
Breathe in...Breathe out.
Breathe in...Breathe out.
You are welcome to take any of the hand placements we practiced in Anchor Breathing.
Begin to notice how your belly rises and falls with your inhales and exhales.
Feel the air moving in and out of your chest.
Become aware of the air as it passes through your nostrils.
Bring your attention to wherever you feel your breath the most, and allow your focus
to reside there.
I will remain silent during this exercise, but when you hear this sound *(play sound of your choice)* bring your attention gently back to your breath.

Wait thirty seconds then play sound.

Wait thirty seconds then play sound.

Wait one minute then play sound.

Wait twenty seconds then play sound.

With your attention still on your breath, slowly begin to wiggle your fingers to bring awareness back to your physical body. When you are ready, open your eyes and notice how you feel.

Day Jumping Hearts

Connecting to the breath and body can be done in stillness, through movement, or through a combination of the two. Today we will work to combine the two experiences.

When we are relaxed, our breath and our heartbeats are slow. When we exercise or experience stress, both our heart rate and breath increase in speed. This is a natural response of the body. Today we will look at how we can use our breath to bring ourselves back to a relaxed state while allowing our heartbeat to slow.

I am going to ask you to jump up and down for thirty seconds. Then you will sit down and place a hand over your heart and begin to take deep breaths to feel your heartbeat slow down.

Please stand up and be mindful of how you are jumping so that you are not bouncing in anyone's space.

Ready...
Set...
Jump!

Time for thirty seconds and stop.

Sit down and place your hand over your heart. Notice how fast it is beating. Take deep, long breaths, and feel your heartbeat begin to slow underneath your hands.

Repeat this activity one to two more times with the option to extend time spent jumping.

Day Anchor Breath and Heartbeat

Today we will combine the concepts explored in Anchor Breathing and Jumping Hearts. This exercise is a bit more challenging, as it asks you to be more mindful of things that are more subtle. I know you are up for the challenge. Do your best to stay present during this activity, and remember to gently bring your attention back to the task at hand as many times as you need.

Begin in your comfortable seated posture. If you are comfortable doing so, please close your eyes. If not, please take your gaze down to help eliminate distractions.

Begin by bringing your attention to the breath. Bring your hands to wherever feels best for you in Anchor Breathing.

Remind students of possible hand placements if needed. Hands in lap, hands on belly, hand on belly and heart, or hand under the nose.

Now, turn your attention to the sound of your breath.
It will likely be very faint and soft.
Can you hear the inhales come in, and the exhales release?

Pause for fifteen seconds.

Now turn your attention to your heartbeat.
Can you feel your heartbeat in your chest?
Maybe you can even hear your heartbeat.

Pause for thirty seconds.

Notice the places your body makes contact with the chair beneath you.

Pause for ten seconds.

Notice the texture of your clothing against your skin.

Pause for ten seconds.

Notice the sounds that exist around you.

Pause for ten seconds.

And then come back to your heartbeat.

Pause for ten seconds.

Now, come back to your breath, noticing it at your anchor.

Pause for ten seconds.

Breathe in, breathe out.
Breathe in, breathe out.
Breathe in, breathe out.

Just notice how you feel. Notice all of the things that you can become aware of in any given moment that you usually miss. Slowly open your eyes.

Day   What Calms Me Down?

Focused breathing, Yoga Naps, and yoga poses are really effective ways to help promote a peaceful mind and body. However, there are countless other ways we can slow down our busy minds to help us relax. Any strategy that calms our bodies and minds can be used as a Proactive or Reactive Stress Management tool. We discussed Proactive and Reactive Stress Management on Day Fifty-Three. Who remembers what these are?

Take a response or two.

Proactive Stress Management is the activities we do on a daily, weekly, or monthly basis that help us be our best selves. This includes eating healthy, exercising, being with friends, etc.

Reactive Stress Management techniques are the ones that we do when we are already feeling stressed to help us to relax.

Please take out your journals or notebook paper. Turn back, or think back, to the list you created on the day we discussed stress management techniques. Take the next few minutes to identify your top three things you can do to help calm yourself down when you feel anxious, sad, or stressed. Maybe you have new items to add based on what we have been practicing. Then, do the same thing for your list of Proactive Stress Management techniques and identify your top three things you do to take care of yourself daily or weekly.

Give students a few minutes to write. Offer an opportunity to share so that students can hear what others do.

Day Anchoring with the Five Senses

When we experience stress or anxiety, our minds often feel like they are racing. At these times, we struggle to slow our thoughts down enough to find peace in our minds and bodies.

Today we will explore a very powerful anchoring activity using our five senses to bring us back to the present moment. We will work through each of our senses in a five, four, three, two, one method; looking for five things we can see, four things we can feel, three things we can hear, two things we can smell, and one thing we are grateful for. When you get to each item, notice it, label it in your mind, and then move onto the next.

Begin by finding your comfortable seated position. Close your eyes for three full deep breaths, and bring your awareness to the present moment.

Inhale...Exhale.
Inhale...Exhale.
Inhale...Exhale.

Slowly open your eyes and notice five things you can see. These can be anything, like a pen or mark on the floor, or it can be the light filtering in the room. Label these items in your mind as you notice each one.

Pause for a few seconds.

Notice four things you can feel. Maybe it's the temperature of the air in the room, the texture of your clothing against your skin, or the hardness of the chair beneath you.

Pause for a few seconds.

Bring your attention to three things you can hear around you. Maybe you can hear your own breath or sounds outside of the room.

Pause for a few seconds.

Notice two things you can smell. Maybe you can still notice the smell of your shampoo or the smells from the hallway.

Pause for a few seconds.

Think of one thing you are grateful for. Maybe it is a person or a place.

Pause for a few seconds.

This exercise is something you can do if you are feeling overwhelmed. Using your five senses helps to ground you and become more present to your surroundings. This exercise can also be practiced to help you be more grateful for the amazing things happening around you. All you need to do is pause and connect to your senses!

Day **Gratitude Rampage**

This activity requires the use of a timer or a clock to keep track of time.

Over the next few days we will return to the idea of gratitude. Who remembers some of the benefits of practicing gratitude?

Take a few responses.

Possible answers: More positive feelings and emotions, better sleep, expressing more kindness and empathy, having stronger immune systems, stronger relationships.

Today we will begin by practicing a Gratitude Rampage. To do this, you will sit with a partner and go back and forth naming items you are grateful for as quickly as you can for thirty seconds. Take a few moments to either think of, or write down, things you are grateful for.

Students partner up, either on their own or at your discretion.

I am going to set a timer for thirty seconds. While facing each other, you will share your gratitude back and forth with one another as quickly as you can. Whoever is the shortest of the partners will go first. Ready, Set, Gratitude!

Time for thirty seconds and stop.

This time, I am going to challenge you. You will share your gratitudes again, but the things you are grateful for need to be bigger than this room. Take a moment to think about that. It could be something like the ocean or an airport. What are things larger than this room you can be grateful for?

Give students time to think of responses.

Ready, Set, Gratitude!

Time for thirty seconds and stop.

Since you did such a great job with that, we are going to add one more challenge. When you share gratitude this time, share only things you are grateful for that are smaller than the palm of your hand. Perhaps you think of a piece of chocolate or your favorite pair of socks.

Give students time to think.

Ready, Set, Gratitude!

Time for thirty seconds and stop.

You are welcome to add in more "challenges" if you have time. Examples: gratitude for non-material items, things you cannot see right now, things in this room, people, etc.

The best thing about this exercise is that it always makes everyone smile! I invite you to practice this at home with family or friends.

Day **68**   Gratitude Journal

This activity involves the use of paper/journal and a writing utensil.
Instruct students to take out their papers and writing utensils.

We can pause and practice gratitude anytime and anywhere! I am going to provide you with specific prompts to help you to express gratitude. This activity helps to increase your self-esteem, improves your quality of life, and offers positive reframing of things we tend to think negatively about. When we look for the positive, we will find it! Please take out your journals and do your best to think of at least three items for each prompt.

Feel free to write these on the board, or read them aloud. You are welcome to offer examples as listed.

I am grateful for my body because...
• the ability to talk, strength to do the things I want to, tasting and digesting all of my favorite foods, the ability to listen to my favorite music, arms to hug people I love.

I am grateful for my mind because...
• keeping me safe in dangerous situations, creative problem solving, coming up with funny jokes.

I am grateful for my community because...
• the police that keep me safe, my favorite restaurant, the basketball court at the park, .

I am grateful for my school because...
• my favorite teacher, the opportunity to take different classes, feeding me every day.

Opportunity for whole group sharing or partner discussion.

Day Gratitude Scavenger Hunt

This activity can take place in your classroom. If possible, however, take your students outside. Determine where you will take students for this activity before you begin.

A Gratitude Scavenger Hunt is just like any other scavenger hunt in that we will be walking around "hunting" for items. I am going to give you five things to look for. If you can only remember three of them, that is okay. You are welcome to write these down to help you remember. When we are "hunting", please stay quiet so you can focus on finding your gratitude.

Take students to their scavenger hunt space.

There is no need to collect these items; just remember them in your mind. We will circle up at the end to share some of the items you found.

- Something that makes you smile.
- Something that is useful to you.
- Something that is your favorite color.
- Something you love the smell of.
- Something that is older than you that you are grateful for.

Bring students back together as a group. Go through each of the items and ask for examples of their findings.

This lesson can be adapted to communicate gratitude in any way that aligns with your school and/or classroom policies. The goal is for each student to extend gratitude to someone else.

It feels amazing to pause and find things we are grateful for, and it is even better when we can share our gratitude with others. There is a proverb that says, "Happiness when shared, is doubled." This means that when we share our happiness with others, we create more happiness in the world.

I invite you to think of someone you are really grateful for; maybe it is a parent, friend, coach, former teacher, principal, or family member. In whatever way is most appropriate for you to communicate, you will express the gratitude you have for them. In a digital or hand-written note, please tell this person that you are grateful for them and offer one, or many, of the reasons why.

If you are choosing to reach out to a friend, maybe you send them a text. If it is a current teacher, send them an email; or if it is a former teacher, maybe you even write them a little letter. Your note can say something like:

- I am grateful to you for being a great friend to me.
- I am grateful that you always cook me dinner.
- I am grateful for all of your patience.
- I am grateful that you are in my life because…
- I am grateful that you push me to be the best version of myself.

Allow students time to extend their gratitude to someone. Monitor their messages and electronics as you see fit.

Day Whole Class Gratitude Rampage

This activity requires the use of a timer or a clock to keep track of time.

The goal of the Gratitude Rampage with your partner was to share as quickly as possible the things you are thankful for. We are going to try this activity with the whole class today. We will gather in a circle and go around one person at a time to each share something we are grateful for. I will time how long it takes us to go around the entire circle the first time. Each time that follows, we will add a challenge and attempt to beat our best time. Begin by thinking of a few things you are grateful for.

Instruct students to sit down in a circle. Determine who will start the share and set a timer.

I will begin the timer as soon as the first person begins, and end it as soon as the last person in the circle shares. You do not need to say, "I am grateful for…" You can just say what you are grateful for to help save time.

Ready...
    Set...
        Gratitude!

Time the circle; share with students how long it took.

Now we are going to see if we can beat our time. Your added challenge is that you cannot repeat something that has already been said. For example, if someone says, "My friends," you cannot say, "Friends," too. This will require active listening. I suggest thinking of a few things you might be able to say off of the top of your head before we begin.

Determine where the class will begin for the second share. Time the circle; share with students how long it took.

Okay, we have one more challenge to see if we can beat our time. This time, you cannot repeat what anyone else says, and whatever you name has to be something inside this school. Take a minute to think of some of the things in this school you are grateful for.

Determine where the class will begin for the third share. Time the circle; share with students how long it took.

Day 72

Gratitude Jar

This exercise asks for your class to start a Gratitude Jar. Please determine what you would like to use for your jar. It does not need to be a jar at all: You can use a cup, a bin, or any other container you have in your classroom.

Students will also need a small piece of paper and a writing utensil.

In order to remember all that we are grateful for, we are going to create a collective Gratitude Jar in this *(hold out jar or identified object)*. This will be a continual jar, meaning you will be able to write down your gratitudes and place them in the jar at any time OR pull one out and read it whenever you feel you need a pick-me-up throughout the semester. Please tear off a small corner of a piece of paper. Write down something or someone that you are grateful for. We will share these aloud with the class.

Give students time to write their gratitudes.

We will go around the room each saying our gratitude out loud while we put our piece of paper in the jar.

Go around the room, allowing students to share their gratitudes while filling the jar. Feel free to repeat this exercise any day you would like to revisit the Gratitude Jar. If someone does something kind in your classroom or in the school, model pausing for gratitude by writing down their name and their act of kindness and putting it in the jar.

Day Senses at the Beach

Our Yoga Nap is going to take us to the beach today. I invite you to use your imagination and all of your senses in this meditation.

Begin by finding your position for your Yoga Nap. Lie down on your back with your arms by your sides. Allow your shoulders to snuggle behind your heart and your palms to face up toward the sky. Relax the muscles in your lower back as your hips and feet fall apart naturally.

Close your eyes and bring your attention to your breath. Breathe in deeply, and exhale completely. Feel your body and mind begin to relax. Feel comfortable, safe, and at peace.

As you breathe, begin to imagine a warm and sunny day with a gentle breeze. It is a perfect day to visit the beach. Maybe you have been to this beach before, or maybe you have never visited a beach in person yet. This beach can be whatever you want it to be. Use your imagination to build the most beautiful, peaceful, and tranquil place you can imagine.

To get to the beach, you begin walking through a canopy of trees. As you walk through this canopy, you hear the wind rustle through the leaves and feel its cool breeze against your skin. The further you walk on this path, the more clearly you can hear the waves in the distance gently lapping against the shore.

Pause for a few seconds.

As you step out of the trees, you see a beautiful, calming, and serene beach. You can see people in the far distance, but you are the only person nearby, and you are completely safe.

See the vast ocean out in front of you rolling with gentle waves. Observe the sunlight twinkling across the water in front of you. Feel the warm sand underneath your feet as you step closer to the coastline.

Pause for a few seconds.

You walk closer to the water so you can feel the refreshing waves move gently over your feet. A soft smile crosses your face.

Pause for a few seconds.

Feel the peace of this moment. Imagine all of the colors of the ocean with its layers of blue spread out in front of you.

Pause for a few seconds.

Embrace the warmth of the sun on your skin, and notice the soothing sounds of the water and the smell of the fresh ocean breeze. Pause and feel grateful for something here.

Stay here for a moment, noticing everything you can. What else can you see? Maybe there are shells scattered across the beach or a boat in the distance.

Pause for a few seconds.

What else can you hear? Maybe there are birds calling in the sky.

Pause for a few seconds.

What else can you feel?
Do you notice the gentle mist that comes off of the ocean?

Pause for a few seconds.

What can you smell?

Pause for a few seconds.

Everything around you adds to your peace in this moment.
Notice how you feel.

Pause for a few seconds.

Look out at the ocean one more time and lock in your memory what it feels like to be this peaceful. Slowly turn around and walk back toward the canopy of trees, once again feeling the soft sand between your toes. Carry these feelings of warmth, safety, and peace with you as you walk back the way you came in. Know that you can return here in your mind anytime you want to find stillness and tranquility.

Bring your attention back to your breath.
Breathe in fully; exhale completely.
Notice any sounds around you in this room.
Notice the places your body makes contact with the floor beneath you.
Feel yourself continue to relax as you begin to wiggle in your fingers and toes.
Gradually allow this movement to become larger; eventually turning into any stretch you need.
When you are ready, open your eyes.

Day

Creating Your Own Happy Place

This activity involves the use of paper/journal and a writing utensil.
Instruct students to take out their papers and writing utensils.

Yesterday, we visited the beach in our Yoga Nap. The beach is often seen as a comforting, calming, and peaceful place. Today you will get to create your own peaceful place in your journals.

This activity asks you to create a vivid picture of your favorite place by using all of your senses in our 5-4-3-2-1 method. You will get to use this place in upcoming Yoga Naps, and it can be a place you visit in your mind whenever you feel stressed, anxious, or worried.

Take a moment to think about your favorite place in the world. It can be somewhere in nature, like a beach or the mountains, or it can be a comforting place like your house. Maybe your favorite place is at your grandparent's house, your bedroom, or maybe it's a place you have seen on television. The place you create can be somewhere you have been, or it can be somewhere you would like to visit.

Pause for students to think about their happy place. Take a few examples from students.

Now, you will do your best to imagine this place in as much detail as possible. On the left side of your paper write down your five senses, leaving enough room between them for details. You are welcome to add more than the 5-4-3-2-1 method, but please come up with these at a minimum.

Give students time to create their lists. Allow them to share as a whole class or with partners if time allows.

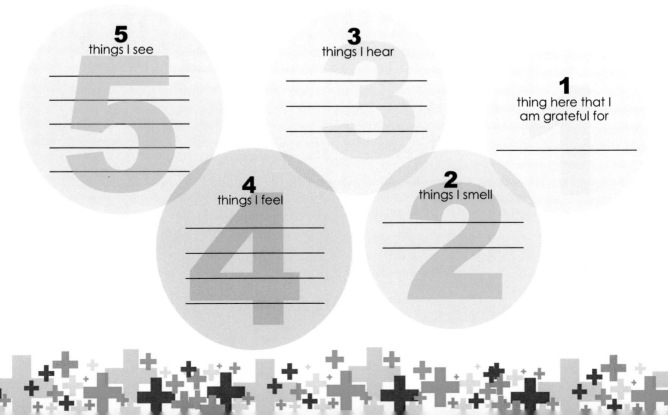

5
things I see
_____
_____
_____
_____

3
things I hear
_____
_____
_____

1
thing here that I
am grateful for
_____

4
things I feel
_____
_____
_____

2
things I smell
_____
_____

Day Visiting Your Happy Place

Today you have the opportunity to visit your own happy place in your Yoga Nap. Begin by finding your position for your Yoga Nap. When you lie on your back with your legs long and arms by your sides, you are sending the message to your brain that it is safe to relax here.

Begin by closing your eyes and just notice how you feel today. Remember, there is no right or wrong way to feel. Just be accepting of yourself and wherever you are today.

Let's take three breaths together:

Inhale 1-2-3
Exhale 3-2-1
Inhale 1-2-3
Exhale 3-2-1
Inhale 1-2-3
Exhale 3-2-1

With your eyes closed, begin to imagine your happy place. Begin by noticing what you see around you. Notice if you are outside or inside. Bring to mind all of the little details you would see there, such as the colors, the objects, or the landscape. Notice if you are alone or with others.

Pause for a few seconds.

Turn your attention now to the things that you can feel here. What is the weather like? Can you feel the clothing against your skin?

Pause for a few seconds.

Listen carefully for the sounds that exist in this space in your mind. Are people talking? Is there music? Is silence the only sound you hear?

Pause for a few seconds.

Everything here is exactly as it should be. All is well, you are right where you are supposed to be. What can you smell? Perhaps it is a sweet treat like cookies baking in the oven. Maybe it is the smell of sweet pine on a crisp morning.

Pause for a few seconds.

Finally, notice something here you are grateful for. Keep this feeling of gratitude with you.

Pause for a few seconds.

Stay here for a few moments, recalling all the details of this space and remembering how you feel.

Show gratitude for your happy place and remember that you can return here in your mind anytime you choose to. This place is always available to you. All you need to do is use your imagination.

Return your attention back to your body, beginning with the breath:

Inhale 1-2-3
Exhale 3-2-1
Inhale 1-2-3
Exhale 3-2-1
Inhale 1-2-3
Exhale 3-2-1

Gently begin to invite small movements back into your body. Become aware how large a small movement can feel when you are relaxed in your body and your mind. Take a good morning stretch, reaching your fingers away from your toes. When you are ready, gently come up into a comfortable seat.

If you are a Language Arts teacher, consider asking students to write a description of their happy place using vivid imagery and details.

Day Sharing Your Happy Place

No two people are exactly alike, yet sometimes we compare ourselves to others. Your strengths and your weaknesses are unique to you. The way you look, talk, think, dress, even the music that you listen to, is all a part of what makes you who you are. As a reminder that we are all wonderfully different, we are going to go around and share our happy places and what we love most about being there. Please remember to be an active listener while your classmates are sharing.

Ask students to go around the room and share their happy places and what they love most about being there.

Sometimes it takes something as simple as hearing what makes someone else happy to remind us we are all unique in our own ways. There is no right or wrong way to be who we are, there is no right or wrong place to be happy, there is no right or wrong way to be happy.

If time allows and you would like to deepen the discussion, ask students to respond to their peers' shares by either expressing something new they learned, something that resonated with them, or something that made them think in a different way.

Day Growth Mindset Intro

This activity involves the use of paper/journal and a writing utensil.
Instruct students to take out their papers and writing utensils.

Over the next few days, we will explore the difference between a Growth Mindset and a Fixed Mindset. Does anyone know the difference between a Growth Mindset and a Fixed Mindset?

Take a few answers.

A Fixed Mindset says that if you are not good at something right now, you will never be good at it. A Growth Mindset, however, believes in the power of "Yet."

The power of "Yet" means that just because you cannot do something right now, it does not mean you will never be able to do it. A Growth Mindset allows us to know that we always have the ability to learn new skills. We might not become masters at everything we try, but a Growth Mindset tells us that we always have the ability to get better and develop our skills in anything we do.

Respond to the following questions in your journals:

What is something you were not good at in the beginning, but you practiced and got better?

What is something you are currently trying to learn?
What is that experience like?
Is it fun and exciting?
Do you get frustrated easily?

How does your Inner Best Friend show up
when you are learning?

How does your Inner Critic show up
when you are learning?

Opportunity for whole class or partner discussion.

THE POWER OF **YET**

Day Growth Mindset Yoga

Yesterday we introduced the concept of a Growth Mindset, and today we will dive a little bit deeper into what it means. Do you remember when you wrote your name with your left hand? It was something new and challenging at the beginning. The same thing probably happened when we tried new yoga poses. Perhaps taking Yoga Naps was hard for you in the beginning, but now you are finding it easier to keep a still body and focus your mind. A Growth Mindset reminds us that, although we might not master everything we set out to learn or do, we can get better at anything if we put forth effort.

Today we are going to do a set series of yoga poses called a Sun Salutation. These poses help to energize us while strengthening and stretching our bodies. Remember the power of "Yet" while we practice this; the more we practice something, the easier it becomes.

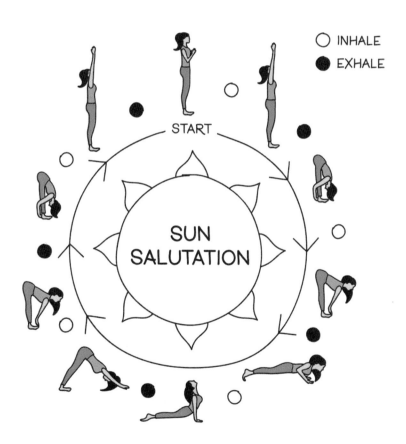

SUN SALUTATION INSTRUCTIONS

- Begin in Mountain Pose with your arms by your side. Stand up tall and proud.
- Inhale, reaching your arms overhead.
- Exhale; put a deep bend in your knees and fold forward, allowing your legs to stretch.
- Bend your knees enough to plant your hands on the ground in front of you. Slowly step one foot back and then the other to come into a Plank Pose.
- Keep your shoulders underneath your wrists: Your lower belly is strong here, and your back is flat.
- Take a deep breath in, and as you exhale, lower yourself all the way to your belly with your elbows hugged in at your sides.
- Inhale; push into your hands and look up to come into Upward Facing Dog.
- Exhale and move into Downward Facing Dog. Lift your hips up high, keep your fingers spread wide, and push your heels down toward the earth.
- Inhale; look between your hands.
- Exhale; step your feet forward to meet your hands and hang down in your Forward Fold.
- Inhale and reach all the way up to Extended Mountain Pose.
- Exhale your hands to your heart center and stand in traditional Mountain Pose.
- Pause and notice how you feel. Notice the thoughts in your mind. Can your Inner Best Friend offer you any advice before we move through this two more times?
- Inhale; reach up overhead.
- Exhale; Forward Fold.
- Inhale and step back to your strong Plank Pose.
- Exhale to slowly lower all the way to the earth.
- Inhale; Upward Facing Dog. Smile! It's just yoga; you don't have to take it so seriously.
- Exhale; Downward Facing Dog.
- Inhale; look up between your hands.
- Exhale; step forward into Forward Fold.
- Inhale; reach up, look up, and lengthen your spine.
- Exhale your hands to your heart.

We will go through this one more time. This time, see if you can remember the sequence of the poses. You can always watch me if you need.

Demonstrate while students move through this on their own.

Mindfulness can actually help us to achieve our goals because it can help us become aware of developing a Growth Mindset. We often have a Fixed Mindset without even being aware of it. However, when we apply our tools of awareness, we can identify moments when our mind is holding us back from trying something new, and we can actively push ourselves out of our comfort zones. In your journals, please reflect on the following question:

What is something that you always wanted to learn to do, but you were afraid of not being good at it, or were afraid of failure?

Please describe this in detail. Then answer these subsequent questions:

- What is a small step you can take in learning how to do this?
- What is a realistic timeline for you to learn how to do this?
- How will you measure your small successes?
- How can you apply the power of "Yet" to this activity?

Day   Growth Mindset Meditation

Please get yourself ready for a Yoga Nap. This Yoga Nap will focus on messages you can offer yourself whenever you are learning a new skill. Get yourself settled on your back with your eyes closed. Do whatever you need in order to feel comfortable and calm in your body.

We are going to begin by taking three deep breaths to the count of three.
Take a deep breath in for 1-2-3,
Let it all out 3-2-1.
Breathe in 1-2-3,
Breathe out 3-2-1.
Breathe in 1-2-3,
Breathe out 3-2-1.
Feel your mind relax and the muscles in your body soften against the floor.
Know that you are safe here.
Know that when we relax, we allow our mental muscles to grow.

Growth Mindset means that you are working toward being the best possible version of yourself. You might not be there YET, but you are working on it.

This means that we find growth through challenges. Sometimes taking a Yoga Nap is a challenge because your mind might start to think about other things or your body might fidget. Just notice if those things happen and continue to work towards being your calmest self in your Yoga Nap.

It is normal for us to shy away from things that are uncomfortable, painful, or hard. But you are facing your challenges! This Mindfulness practice of a Yoga Nap helps you to be the best version of yourself by strengthening your mental muscles! Relax and repeat these phrases in your mind as I say them out loud.

The best version of myself...
sees a challenge, and instead of giving up, offers a positive affirmation such as, "I am strong."

The best version of myself...
believes that I am capable of doing hard things even after I fail at it once, twice, or maybe even three times or more.

The best version of myself...
is always growing and trying.

The best version of myself...
asks for help when I do not understand or something is too challenging.

The best version of myself...
is capable of doing the hard things that help me to grow.

Repeat two times and then pause.

Think back to a time when you struggled with something that you can do really well now! Maybe it was learning a new sport, tackling a new skill in math class, learning to cook, discovering how to ride a bike, or learning to play an instrument. Think about how hard it was to learn that skill in the beginning, and how you did not give up.

Picture yourself in the beginning stages of learning. Picture yourself on one of those days when it was really challenging for you and you wanted to give up. What could you say to yourself to encourage yourself to keep trying?

What feelings did you have when you did not give up even though something was hard? Maybe you felt proud, accomplished, tired, or joyful! Remember this the next time you are faced with something that is hard and you feel like you want to give up.

In order to be the best version of ourselves, we need to believe that we are capable and worthy of accomplishing hard things. Saying kind things to yourself helps you believe in yourself. This part is really important. Whisper these phrases quietly to yourself after I say them out loud.

I am worthy of being treated kindly by myself and others.

I am worthy of doing great things.

I am worthy of being the best version of myself.

Take a few moments to pause and notice how you feel.

Pause for a few seconds.

You have done an amazing job connecting your strong mind, relaxed body, and kind heart. Now begin to wiggle your fingers and toes as you slowly start to bring awareness back to your physical self.

Day   Same Street

Today I am going to read you a short story called "Autobiography in Five Chapters" by Portia Nelson. While I read this story to you, please think about the meaning and symbolism of the story. We will share our thoughts at the end.

ONE
I walk down the street.
There is a deep hole in the sidewalk.
I fall in.
I am lost...

I am hopeless.
It isn't my fault.
It takes forever to find a way out.

TWO
I walk down the same street.
There is a deep hole in the sidewalk.
I pretend I don't see it.
I fall in again.
I can't believe I'm in the same place.
But it isn't my fault.
It still takes a long time to get out.

THREE
I walk down the same street.
There is a deep hole in the sidewalk.
I see it is there.
I still fall in...it's a habit
My eyes are open; I know where I am;
It is my fault.
I get out immediately.

FOUR
I walk down the same street.
There is a deep hole in the sidewalk.
I walk around it.

FIVE
I walk down another street.

Facilitate a discussion around this short story/poem. Talking points can include:
- *What do you think the street symbolizes?*
- *Will the street mean something different to different people?*
- *Why is it easy to make the same mistakes repeatedly?*
- *How does the narrator's experience change throughout the story?*
- *How can you apply the principles of Mindfulness to the story?*

Day Finding Your Center

For this breath practice we will sit on the ground with our legs in a criss-cross position. If this is uncomfortable for your body, you might choose to extend your legs out in front of you. Alternatively, it might feel best for you to kneel. It is important that this activity takes place on the ground instead of seated in your chair because it involves movement that a chair might restrict.

Begin in your seated posture. Feel your sit bones connected to the earth. Relax your hips down toward the floor and straighten your spine. This exercise is called Finding Your Center, and it helps to connect the mind and body by promoting a positive association between the two.

Take several deep breaths and close your eyes. As you inhale, feel your torso expand in all directions; your belly grows forward, there is a small rise in your lower back, and your side body expands laterally. Notice the subtle rise and fall of your chest with your breath and feel a softness to your face and shoulders.

Keep your eyes closed. Remember, you are in a safe space. Take a deep breath in; as you exhale, lean as far to the right as you can without lifting your left hip off of the ground. Inhale and return to your center. Exhale; begin to lean to the left as far as you can without lifting your right hip. Inhale and return to center. We will slowly repeat this process, leaning less and less every time.

Inhale; as you exhale, lean to the right. Inhale and come back to center. Exhale; lean to the left. Inhale back to center, and exhale to the right. Inhale to center, and exhale lean to the left.

Practice this two more times on each side, following your own inhales and exhales. Remember to lessen the movement each time. When you finally reach the middle, find your center with your belly button, heart, and head all in one line. Take several deep breaths here. Again, feel your torso expand in all directions on your inhale, and as you exhale feel everything come back to center.

Notice what it feels like to be in balance. Notice what it feels like to be still. Take one more inhale, and exhale fully. Slowly begin to wiggle in your fingers and open your eyes.

Day Check-In

Today we will repeat an exercise we practiced earlier to check in with our minds, bodies, and emotions. We revisit this check-in because our thoughts, physical sensations in the body, and emotions are always changing. This is an exercise that can be practiced daily, or even multiple times throughout your day.

Find your seated posture. Feel your spine grow tall as you allow your eyes to close or take your gaze down to the ground. We will begin by taking three breaths to come into this moment.

Inhale fully, exhale slowly.
Again; inhale fully, exhale slowly.
Last time; inhale fully, exhale slowly.

Feel your feet pressing into the floor.
Notice the points on your body that make contact with your chair.
Feel the muscles in your face soften and your shoulders drop down naturally.
Begin to notice how you feel today. Remember, that there is no right or wrong answer to how you feel. Mindfulness simply asks us to be aware of how we are feeling without judgement.

Ask yourself the following questions, making space for whatever comes up:

How does my mind feel today?

Pause for a few seconds.

Perhaps you notice your mind is full of thoughts, or your mind is having a hard time focusing. Maybe your mind is relaxed and ready to learn. Remember there is no right answer for how you feel right now.

Pause for a few seconds.

How does my body feel today?

Pause for a few seconds.

Is your body feeling strong today? Energized? Tired? Sore? Maybe there are parts of your body you are more aware of today than others. Just notice sensations in your body.

Pause for thirty seconds.

How am I feeling emotionally today?

Pause

Are you happy? Is there some uncertainty or worry? What general feelings come up?

Pause for thirty seconds.

As you sit and breathe, notice if you have created any judgements around your states of being today. It is okay if you have. Just like Mindfulness, nonjudgement takes time to cultivate.

How you feel mentally, physically, and emotionally is always changing. Knowing that how we feel is always temporary helps us to appreciate the good moments and gives us a healthy perspective on more challenging times.

Breathe with whatever is here for three more breaths, knowing that this will change in maybe five minutes, an hour, or a day. Appreciate what is here, right now.

Inhale fully, exhale slowly.
Again; inhale fully, exhale slowly.
Last time; inhale fully, exhale slowly.

This activity involves the use of paper/journal and a writing utensil.
Instruct students to take out their papers and writing utensils.

Mindfulness allows us to be aware of the thoughts in our minds, sensations in our bodies, and emotions in our hearts. Mindfulness can also help us identify the things in our lives that assist us in being better versions of ourselves, as well as identify the things that might bring about self-doubt or criticism.

Today we are going to look at external influences; ie: people, music, television, friends, books, social media, etc., and how they influence our lives. We can identify when something or someone is a positive influence on our lives based upon the feelings associated with the experiences we have with those people or things. In this way, what we engage with on an external level influences our internal emotions.

In other words, the people you surround yourself with, the shows you watch, and the music you listen to all influence the thoughts and feelings you have about yourself and the world around you.

IN YOUR JOURNAL, PLEASE IDENTIFY THE FOLLOWING:

5 people you admire...
- These can be people you know, celebrities, family members, friends, fictional characters, etc.

5 specific things that inspire you...
- Maybe you can think of a book you read, or music you love. Perhaps it is a story you heard, a television show, a group you follow on social media, a belief system, or an organization.

5 goals you have for yourself...
- Please make these goals realistic and hopeful. Identify something deeper than "getting through the week" or your overall high school career. Challenge yourself a bit here. Do you want to go to college? What would you like to do for work? Do you want to learn how to garden? Is your goal to have a family? These goals could be for five days from now, five years from now, or even fifty years from now.

Day 85 Five People You Spend Time With

Did you know there are different ways to spend time with people? When we think of spending time with someone, we usually think about sitting in a room with them. However, there are countless ways to spend time with a person.

What are some ways you spend time with, or are influenced by, people without actually seeing them?
Possible answers: Text messages, phone calls, all forms of social media, following people on social media, television shows, books, music, etc.

Did you know that the people you spend time with influence who you are? Your energy, outlook, and personality are deeply influenced by the five people you spend most of your time with. Think about this for a moment. Try to think about the people you spend most of your time with. Are they people you want to be like, or aspire to be like? If not, why do you choose to spend time with them? Is it because they are familiar? Do they have something that you want, like popularity or a skill? Is it because they are a family member?

There are a lot of quotes about how your vibe attracts your tribe, but today I ask you to remember that your tribe also impacts your vibe.

In your journals, please identify five to ten people you spend a majority of your time with. Since you live with your parents, for the purpose of this activity, just look at the people you spend your time with when you are not at home. In other words, look at the five to ten people you choose to spend your time with. Take into account that "spending time" with someone can also happen digitally. Therefore, it is important to take into account the people you text with on a regular basis as well.

Give students time to journal. You are welcome to facilitate a conversation around how to be mindful about who we spend our time with.

Day   Five People You Admire

We have been working to bring mindful awareness to ourselves about the people we spend our time with, and how they can help us or hurt us in our own growth and evolution.

Two days ago, you identified five people you admire. Today, you are invited to examine the qualities you admire about them. We know that the people we spend time with - whether in person, through messages, or by reading their books - influence us. Therefore, it is important that we pay close attention to their positive qualities. Looking at the positive qualities in others is a way for us to discover and strengthen our own values.

Please take out your journals and turn to the list of the five people you admire. For each individual, write down three positive qualities they possess. Some examples of positive qualities are a strong work ethic, honesty, positivity, compassion, loyalty, and open-mindedness. When we are finished, we will go around the room and share one quality that we have identified we admire. You will have the option to say the person's name or simply share the quality.

Allow students time to identify three qualities for each of their five people. When they are finished, go around the room and ask each student to share one of the qualities they admire. They are welcome to share the name of the person with this quality, or simply offer the quality itself.

OPTIONAL DISCUSSION: *What should we do if we cannot identify positive qualities in someone? What role should we allow these people to have in our lives?*

Day **87** Visualizing Your Dream

This activity involves the use of paper/journal and a writing utensil.
Instruct students to take out their papers and writing utensils.

Hopefully by now you recognize that your mind is a very powerful place. Your mind has the ability to work with you or against you--it all depends on what you allow it to do. We have worked to improve our ability to concentrate, build compassion towards ourselves and others, strengthen our Inner Best Friends, and so much more. Today we will use something called visualization as a way to help you achieve your goals. A visualization takes place when you picture something in your mind with great detail.

Can you think of anyone that uses visualizations to help them succeed?

Take a few answers.

Anyone working toward a goal, no matter what it is, can use visualization. This includes an athlete imagining themselves in the midst of a championship celebration holding a trophy, someone visualizing their dream home or vacation with attention to detail, or imagining yourself walking across the stage at graduation. Anyone can use visualization to help them on their journey towards something they want, including you!

In your journals, you identified five goals you have. Please choose one of your identified goals and write down as many details as you can about what it will look like and feel like once you achieve this goal. Think back to all of the imagery you included in your happy place visualization and try to incorporate all five senses here as well. Feel free to write down whatever else you would like to about this goal and what it will feel like to accomplish it.

Offer students the opportunity to share their visions with someone seated near them.

Day Guided Visualization of Your Dream

Today we are going to participate in a Yoga Nap that utilizes a visualization of yourself as you achieve your dream. Many successful people say they use visualization as an important part of their journey in achieving their goals. If you would like to open your journal and review what you wrote down yesterday, please take a moment to do so. When you are finished, get yourself set up for your Yoga Nap.

Lie on your back with your arms by your sides and begin to let yourself settle in. Know that you are safe and supported here. Feel your mind settle down as you close your eyes, and feel your body settle as you begin to focus on your breath moving deep down into your belly. Feel your emotions settle as you begin to relax your body and your mind. As I count down from five, begin to visualize your dream coming true to the fullest extent possible.

5...as you breathe in, imagine that you are taking your first deep conscious inhale just after accomplishing your goal or dream.

Pause for ten seconds.

4...look around you and notice your surroundings as you have achieved your goal. Are you by yourself? Are you surrounded by a crowd of people? Are you with just a few loved ones?

Pause for ten seconds.

3...notice the space you are in. Are you in nature? A large event hall? Are you on a stage? Is it a quiet moment from your bed? What does the space look like? Can you imagine all of the colors from the floor to the ceiling? What does the space smell like? What scents do you notice?

Pause for ten seconds.

2...notice what sounds you hear. Is there clapping? Silence? Cheering? Maybe there is a song playing in the background.

Pause for ten seconds.

1...notice how you feel. What will it feel like when you accomplish this dream? Notice how it feels in each part of your body. Feel the warmth that radiates from your heart, or the sense of pride that exists in your smile. Live in this feeling, settle into this feeling, and allow yourself to reside here for the next few moments.

Pause for at least one minute for your students to reside here.

Begin to bring awareness back into your body as I count from one to five.

1...notice the feeling of warmth in your heart and in your belly. Keep this feeling of warmth with you.

Pause for ten seconds.

2...open your ears to any sounds that exist in the room. Maybe that sound is simply the sound of silence.

Pause for ten seconds.

3...feel the places on your body that make contact with the floor. These might be your hips, shoulders, the backs of your hands, and your head.

Pause for ten seconds.

4...begin to gently bring movement back to your body by wiggling your fingers and your toes. Make small circles with your wrists and ankles or bring other small movements back into your body.

Pause for ten seconds.

5...rock your head back and forth, and when you are ready, take a beautiful good morning stretch.

Pause for ten seconds.

In your own time, gently roll onto one side, and then bring yourself up to a seated position.

Day Beliefs About Myself

This activity involves the use of paper/journal and a writing utensil.
Instruct students to take out their papers and writing utensils.

You have the ability to achieve your dreams. You possess more intelligence, strength, and gifts than you know. In order to accomplish something that you truly desire, you must believe three things.

First, you need to believe in yourself. Second, you need to believe you are worthy of accomplishing your dreams. And lastly, you will need to work hard towards achieving your goals.

This is much easier said than done. However, it is necessary for us to do these things in order to have the lives that we want. Today's journal exercise asks you to be really honest with yourself. This exercise is important because we will look at our own beliefs about ourselves.

Mindfulness reminds us that when we become aware of something, we have the ability to embrace it if it is beneficial. Conversely, we have the power to change our own thinking if we find it is hindering our progress and growth.

Please answer the following questions about yourself:
- What beliefs do I hold about myself?
- Are my thoughts about myself empowering and positive, or limiting and negative?
- What is something that helps me to believe in myself?
- Who are people that help me believe in myself?
- What are things I do that make me feel good? How can I spend more time doing these things?

Day **What I Like About Myself**

*This activity involves the use of paper/journal and a writing utensil.
Instruct students to take out their papers and writing utensils.*

It is very easy for us to say negative things about ourselves, either out loud or in our heads. It can also be uncomfortable to hear nice things someone else has to say about us. Today, you will explore positive things about yourselves and practice speaking them out loud. You will hear positive statements about yourself from a partner as well.

For this activity, you will write down five things you enjoy or appreciate about yourself, and three things you enjoy or appreciate about your partner. Then, the two of you will sit together. Partner One will share three of the five positive things they identified about themselves, and Partner Two will share the three things they like about Partner One. After Partner One is finished, Partner Two will share three things they appreciate about themselves, and Partner One will read the three things they appreciate Partner Two.

Students divide into pairs. You may choose to assign partners, although since this is a personal activity, it might feel best for students to choose their own.

In your journals, please write down five things you really enjoy about yourself. Maybe you choose to challenge yourself to find one physical attribute, one emotional characteristic, one moral or value, one personality trait, and one skill you have. Then, please write down three things you appreciate or admire about your partner.

Allow time for students to create their lists.

Please meet with your partner and sit across from them. Do your best to make eye contact with them and actually listen to what they say about themselves and what they say about you. Be mindful about how you feel during this activity.

Have partners play a round of rock, paper, scissors, to determine who goes first. This will alleviate some of the nervous energy.

After the groups are complete you are welcome to simply end the exercise, or have students complete one of the following activities:

1 • *Have students reflect in their journals about the experience using the following guiding questions: What was it like to say things I appreciate about myself? What was it like to hear someone else say things they appreciate about me? Was there anything that surprised me?*

2 • *Facilitate a whole-class discussion about the activity and its impact.*

Day 01 Metta Mindfulness

This activity requires the use of a timer or a clock to keep track of time.

We have the power to use our thoughts to think positive thoughts for ourselves, as well as to send positive thoughts out for others. There is a practice called Metta Mindfulness that uses four phrases to send good wishes to ourselves and others. All you need in order to practice Metta is the ability to picture people in your mind, just like in your guided visualization, and these four phrases:

May you be happy.
May you be healthy.
May you feel loved.
May you be safe.

These phrases are well wishes, and can be applied to anyone at any time. During our practice today, you will send these wishes to four different people. The first person you will send these thoughts to is yourself. When you begin the practice of Metta Mindfulness, you always start by offering these thoughts or well wishes to yourself because it is important that you feel happy, healthy, loved, and safe before you can offer those same things to others.

The second person you will send Metta to is someone you love very much, such as a family member, friend, or even a pet. The third person you will send Metta to is someone you have neutral feelings towards, such as a person you saw at the grocery store or an acquaintance that you don't know on a very deep level.

Finally, the fourth person you will send Metta to is the most challenging, but it is also the most important. The last person you will send positive wishes to is someone who has been difficult for you to get along with or be around. Sending well wishes to someone we do not like very much is the most important because oftentimes the people who are unkind to us act this way because they do not feel they are liked - they do not feel happy, healthy, loved, or safe.

For the purpose of this exercise, however, please do not try to send your Metta wishes to the person you have the hardest time liking or getting along with. That is something we all must work up to over time! Perhaps it will feel good to start small, by thinking of someone who was accidently unkind to you one time, or once said something negative about you. Maybe this person has apologized, or maybe they have not; you still have the power to think good thoughts for them. While it is not okay for someone to mistreat you, you have the ability to offer kindness and compassion to anyone you choose.

Begin in your comfortable seated position with a tall spine. When you are ready, close your eyes. Take a deep inhale through your nose, and back out through your nose. Inhale deeply again, and exhale fully.

Bring to mind a picture of yourself. Maybe visualize yourself right here and now, maybe imagine a picture of yourself doing an activity you love, or maybe picture yourself as a child... visualize that image of yourself and repeat these four phrases in your mind a I say them outloud:

May I be happy.
May I be healthy.
May I feel loved.
May I be safe.
Repeat

Now, bring to mind a picture of someone you love very much. Think of someone who makes you smile the moment you think of them. With that person in your mind, visualize that you are saying these phrases to this person as I say them out loud.

May you be happy.
May you be healthy.
May you feel loved.
May you be safe.
Repeat

Think of a person in your life that you have neutral feelings towards. It might even be a person you passed on your drive on the way to school. We send good thoughts to this person to remember that we can offer kindness to anyone, even people we do not know very well.

May you be happy.
May you be healthy.
May you feel loved.
May you be safe.
Repeat

It is so important to practice Metta on ourselves and people we love. Now we will practice the most challenging and most important part of Metta; sending love to someone who is difficult to like. Bring to mind a picture of someone who is hard to love right now. Maybe you can try to imagine this person smiling, as it is hard to stay mad at someone when we see them smile. To the best of your ability, send kindness to this person while repeating these phrases in your mind as I say them outloud.

May you be happy.
May you be healthy.
May you feel loved.
May you be safe.
Repeat

Pause for a moment and notice how you feel. We often feel better and act with more kindness to those around us after we use this exercise. You can do this activity for yourself and for others anytime you wish. Bring your attention back to the room by deepening your breath.

Take a deep inhale through your nose, and back out through your nose.
Inhale deeply, and exhale fully.
Slowly open your eyes.

Day Group Tree

Our thoughts and actions impact ourselves and those around us. To demonstrate this, we will practice Tree Pose. Tree Pose is a balance pose that requires focus, strength, and stability. We can practice these things by ourselves, with someone else, or in a large group. Today, we will do all three.

Begin in your Mountain Pose with your feet beneath your hips. Stand with a tall spine and relax the muscles in your face, especially in your jaw. In your mind, think the following phrases; "I am focused, I am strong, I am stable."

Begin to shift your weight into your right leg and lift your left heel off of the ground. Open your left hip up out to the side and create a kick stand with your left foot and right inner ankle.

You are welcome to stay here, or bring the sole of the left foot to the inside of the right calf or the inside of the right thigh. Remember to use one focal point in front of you that is not moving to help focus your mind and balance your body. You are welcome to grow your tree by extending your arms up over your head, or place them at heart center. Take a full breath in your Tree Pose.

Gently exit the posture in reverse of the way you came in; release your arms by your side, pull your left knee back to center, and slowly lower your foot down to the earth.

Find your Mountain Pose again. Breathe in fully, and exhale completely. Let's try the other side.

Find your focal point with your eyes and repeat the following phrases in your mind; "I am focused, I am strong, I am stable."

Shift your weight into your left leg and take the weight out of your right toes. Even though you just practiced this pose while standing on your right leg, it is normal for any pose in yoga to feel completely different on one side compared to the other.

See which leg variation feels good for you on this side; either place your right foot into a kickstand, the right foot on the left calf, or the right foot on the left inner thigh. Play around with which arm variation feels good for you and remember to breathe.

Slowly and with control, begin to lower your arms down. Bring your left knee back to the centerline of the body, lower your foot to the floor, and come into Mountain Pose.

Now we are going to see what happens when we find Tree Pose with a partner. *(You may choose to assign partners or allow them to choose)*

Stand side-by-side with your partner, both of you facing the same direction. The partner on the left will balance on their right leg to start, and the partner on the right will balance on their left leg to start.

Slowly begin to find your Tree Pose standing next to your partner. When you both feel balanced in your legs, reach your arms up to shoulder height with your palms facing out. See if you can touch palms with your inner hands. You might feel yourself sway as your partner sways, or you might feel even more balanced than usual. Take three breaths balanced with your partner like this.

Demonstrate and pause.

When you have completed your three breaths, switch sides so the partner on the left becomes the partner on the right. This will allow you to switch the legs you were balancing on. If you want to test your balance together, see if you can leave your inner arms down by your sides and side stretch to touch palms with your outer arms. Take three breaths with your partner and slowly lower down.

Now, we will all come into a big circle to make a circle of trees. When we balanced with our partners, we felt how one person can positively or negatively impact another's balance. This is taken to an even bigger scale when we are with a larger group.

To make our circle of trees, when you come into Tree Pose, you will reach both arms up to touch palms with the people on either side of you. Let's all begin balancing on the right leg. First start by taking your eyes to a focal point that is not moving to aid your balance and focus. When you are ready, get light on your left toes and find a variation of Tree Pose that feels good.

On the count of three, everyone lift your arms up to shoulder height and touch hands with the people next to you. Notice how if one person sways, it impacts the whole group. We can use our circle of trees to help hold one another up. It is okay if you fall out--just get back up again and rejoin the group. Let's see if we can all hold this for three breaths.

Repeat this on the other side.

This exercise is an excellent reminder of how much we impact one another and how we can support each other. Great job!

Day **93** "Maybe"

As humans, we have the tendency to want to control what is happening around us. However, most of the things we experience in life are out of our control. We cannot control what the weather is like, who our family members are, how others behave, what happened in the past, or what will happen in the future.

When we focus our attention on the things we cannot control, it leads to feelings of helplessness, anxiety and despair. However, there is one thing we always have control over--we have the ability to choose how we respond to anything and everything that happens in our lives. Knowing that we can choose how we respond to events in our lives makes all the difference.

Mindfulness plays a huge role in this because mindfulness is the pause between the action (what happens to us) and our reaction (how we respond to it). When something upsetting happens, it is natural to want to react. Reactions look different for everyone; some react by yelling, crying, shutting down, complaining, or avoiding.

However, we can apply our mindfulness practice in these moments by stopping and checking in to ask, "How am I feeling right now (physically, mentally, and emotionally)?" Furthermore, we can ask ourselves, "How would I like to respond to this situation?"

The following is a Taoist story about an old farmer. As you listen, please see where he could have reacted, and possible reasons why he chose to respond the way that he did. We will discuss this as a class at the end.

There was an old farmer who had worked his crops for many years. One day his horse ran away. Upon hearing the news, his neighbors came to visit. "Such bad luck," they said sympathetically.

"Maybe," the farmer replied.

The next morning the horse returned, bringing with it three other wild horses. "How wonderful!" the neighbors exclaimed.

"Maybe," replied the old man.

The following day, the farmer's son tried to ride one of the untamed horses. He was thrown off the horse and broke his leg. The neighbors again came to offer their sympathy for what they called his misfortune. "What terrible luck," they said.

"Maybe," answered the farmer.

The day after, military officials came to the village to draft young men into the army. Seeing that the son's leg was broken, they passed him by. The neighbors congratulated the farmer on how well things had turned out for him.

"Maybe," said the farmer.

Open class discussion about the story. Possible talking points:
1 • *Is anything in life all good or all bad?*
2 • *Why do you think the farmer only responded with, "Maybe"?*
3 • *How can you apply this story and its teachings to your own life?*

Day Practicing Pause

This activity involves the use of paper/journal and a writing utensil.
Instruct students to take out their papers and writing utensils.

Yesterday, we learned that Mindfulness is the pause between action and reaction. It is important to note that in this situation, an action is something that happens to you, whereas reaction is how you choose to respond. Any action can have a positive or negative influence in your immediate life, as can your response to it.

Practicing the pause between action and reaction is a lifelong skill. Oftentimes, it is after we react to a situation that we realize we could have done something differently. This is completely normal and natural. Looking at past reactions is a good starting place to consider possible future responses to life events.

In your journal, you will reflect on one event from your past when you had a strong reaction, and write about how you might respond differently to a similar event in the future. This is Mindfulness in action! Please remember to apply all the principles of Mindfulness we have been practicing, especially non-judgement of ourselves, as everyone struggles with reactions and responses.

Please take out your journal and identify:

- One instance in the past when you reacted without pausing.
  EXAMPLE: a disagreement with a sibling, getting a poor grade, getting sick, etc.
- One instance in the future when you want to intentionally pause before reacting.
  EXAMPLE: the next time your parent says something that upsets you, an upcoming presentation, getting a message from a friend that makes you feel unvalued.
- One way you can apply the "Maybe" principle from the Taoist story.

We can not always choose what **HAPPENS TO US**
But we can **+ ALWAYS**
choose how we **RESPOND** to what
HAPPENS TO US

Day Unitask

We live in a very fast-paced world where we are used to doing multiple things at once; eating while driving, texting and walking, watching television while doing homework, etc.

Multitasking is the act of doing multiple things at once, usually in an attempt to save time. Studies show that multitasking actually decreases productivity and creativity, and increases the number of mistakes we make and our levels of anxiety.

When we are trying to multitask, it is nearly impossible to practice Mindfulness and reap its benefits. Unitasking is the practice of focusing attention on one task at a time. It is a very practical mindful activity.

With the right mindset, you can focus on any single task at once. An example of this would be while cleaning up from dinner that you just focus on the tasks needed to clean, rather than thinking about the homework assignment you have to complete later. Or, when you shower, you really bring your awareness to where you are and what you are doing - focus on the sensation of the water against your skin and the smell of your soap. Unitasking can be very uncomfortable for many people at first because multitasking has become the norm in our present society.

Allow students to choose a partner or assign partners.

With a partner, please come up with two possible ways you can unitask today. When we are finished, each pair will share with the class one way they are committed to unitasking today.

Give students time to meet with their partners to discuss, then offer opportunity for a whole class discussion.

Day   The Art of Being

This activity asks for you to play a song of your choice for students to listen to in a Yoga Nap. Feel free to choose your own relaxing song, or choose one from the following suggestions:

"Be Here Now" by Ray LaMontange
"Breathing Space" by Sacred Earth
"So Long, Lonesome" by Explosions in the Sky

Most of our days are spent in constant motion. This means we spend very little time just being and not doing. Even when we say we are "doing nothing", we are usually doing something like scrolling on our phones or watching television.

It is important to set goals, work hard, and strive to be the best version of ourselves. However, it is equally as important that we offer ourselves time to not do anything so we can remember how to relax and to unitask. Our Yoga Naps are a great example of "being" instead of "doing." Today, we will integrate unitasking and the art of being by lying down for a Yoga Nap and listening to a song.

Begin by making yourself comfortable for your Yoga Nap. Lie with your arms long by your sides or with your hands on your belly. Allow your legs to extend straight in front of you. You may choose to close your eyes or keep them open for this practice. Your job, right now, is simply to allow yourself to be.

Find peace in knowing there is nothing you need to do right now. Take a deep breath in and relax as you exhale all the way out. Breathe in deeply, and exhale completely. Repeat this one more time taking the deepest breaths of your day so far. Remember that it is normal for your mind to begin thinking about other things. If you notice that your mind wanders off during our Yoga Nap, gently bring your awareness back to the music. Allow yourself to just be here, relaxing and listening to the song. There is nothing you need to do right now. There is no right or wrong way to complete this exercise. Just be.

Play song of your choice.

Begin to bring your awareness back to your body on the floor. Acknowledge any thoughts that came up during this practice. Acknowledge any feelings that came up during this practice. Finally, acknowledge any sensations in the body that came up.

Slowly begin to wiggle your fingers and toes. Allow the movement to gradually get larger, offering yourself any stretch that feels good. When you are ready, gently come back to a seated position.

This is something you can practice anytime you need a pause; whether you find a song to play, a guided relaxation to listen to, or just set a timer in your Yoga Nap or seated posture.

Day   Peace of Mind

Hopefully you have begun to pause and check in with how you feel mentally, physically, and emotionally on a more regular basis. When challenging thoughts or feelings come up, it is common to feel some resistance in dealing with them because they are uncomfortable.

Humans have a tendency to avoid negative thoughts and feelings by pretending they are not there. Today we will focus on ways to deal with your thoughts and feelings as they arise, whatever they might be.

Begin in your comfortable position for a seated practice. Sit up tall and proud, without having too much resistance or rigidity in your shoulders and spine. When you are ready, close your eyes.

Breathe in 1-2-3
Breathe out 3-2-1
Breathe in 1-2-3
Breathe out 3-2-1
Breathe in 1-2-3
Breathe out 3-2-1

Bring your attention to your heart. Maybe you can imagine your breath sending fresh oxygen to your physical, beating heart.

Breathe in 1-2-3
Breathe out 3-2-1

Maybe you can imagine your breath creating space inside of your emotional heart.

Breathe in 1-2-3
Breathe out 3-2-1

Ask yourself, "How am I feeling emotionally today?" Notice what feelings arise while keeping your focus on your heart center. Maybe you feel joy, sadness, fear, excitement, heaviness, lightness. Maybe you are having a hard time connecting with any sensation at all. That is okay too.

Breathe in 1-2-3
Breathe out 3-2-1

We will work through some steps to help us accept whatever emotions are present inside ourselves. These steps can be applied right now in this seated practice, as well as any other time you need them.

First, acknowledge whatever feelings you are having right now.

Breathe in 1-2-3
Breathe out 3-2-1

Second, accept that the feeling is there. Remember, feelings are never good or bad. Feelings are not facts. They just are.

Breathe in 1-2-3
Breathe out 3-2-1

Third, recognize your thoughts and feelings are there for a reason. Everyone on this earth experiences a wide range of thoughts and emotions at different times in their lives. You are no different.

Breathe in 1-2-3
Breathe out 3-2-1

Fourth, remember this feeling is not forever. Just like events in life, thoughts and feelings are always changing.

Breathe in 1-2-3
Breathe out 3-2-1

Fifth, ask yourself the deeper questions such as, "Why am I feeling this way? What do I need at this moment?"

Breathe in 1-2-3
Breathe out 3-2-1

Sixth, allow this feeling to be here with you right now. Allow yourself to feel whatever it is you are feeling. Know that you are safe, you have resources, and your present situation is always changing.

Breathe in 1-2-3
Breathe out 3-2-1

Bring your attention back from your heart to your breath. Take two of these counting breaths on your own, and when you are finished, open your eyes.

Day Why Practice Mindfulness

This activity involves the use of paper/journal and a writing utensil.
Instruct students to take out their papers and writing utensils.

You have learned so much about Mindfulness so far. As a class, we are going to review some of the items you have learned and compile a list of reasons to continue to practice Mindfulness.

Allow students to work in partners first, or begin as a large group.

Let's begin by defining Mindfulness. What components of Mindfulness can you remember?
Possible answers:
- Awareness
- Being in the present moment
- Nonjudgement
- Pausing between an action and reaction

Great! Now that you know what it is, what are some of the benefits of practicing Mindfulness?
Possible answers:
- Increases concentration and focus
- Improves overall health
- Increases positivity
- Increases overall satisfaction with life
- Increases ability to stay calm
- Increases memory
- Improves creativity

We know there are countless ways to practice Mindfulness. We can use Mindfulness when we do anything from lying down to take a Yoga Nap to driving a car. What are some of your favorite ways to practice Mindfulness?

Allow students to provide answers.

In your journals reflect on:
- Three benefits you felt after practicing Mindfulness yourself
- Two things you learned about yourself
- One goal you have in using Mindfulness

Day You Are a Gift • By Anne Funke

Today's Yoga Nap is designed to remind you that you are amazing just because you are you. There is nobody else in the world who looks like you, thinks like you, talks like you, or has the same experiences as you. All of these things make you uniquely who you are.

Get yourself settled for a Yoga Nap by lying down on your back and making your body and mind as relaxed as possible.

Lie quietly and close your eyes. Breathe evenly to quiet your mind.

Pause for a few seconds.

You are a gift. You are important, loved, and valued. Absolutely nothing can take away your worth. Many times, these words are difficult to believe about ourselves. This is particularly true when we make mistakes, say unkind things to people we care about, or are the ones who are hurt by words and actions. At these times, we second guess ourselves and our choices, and it can feel like everyone and everything is better than we are.

This is simply not true. You have more kindness, love, and light inside you than you know. Your strengths...and gifts...and abilities...make you uniquely you. That is something no one can take away. What you do, and think and feel, matters more than you'll ever know. Be kind to yourself. We are all just human, and that's good enough. All the things you think make you not enough are exactly what's needed in this world. You are enough.

Pause and go through this next part slowly.

You are enough. You are worthy. You are valuable. You are important. You are precious. You are a gift. You are enough.

As you listen to these affirmations, which one might you need most today? Repeat that to yourself as you lie still and breathe. Maybe another word comes to mind that you're needing right now in this space. Repeat that to yourself as you lie still and breathe.

Pause for thirty seconds.

Start to bring your awareness back into the room and to the people in this room with you. How does it feel to know that all of us, right now, are repeating these powerful words to ourselves? We are each a gift and we are each so valuable and worthy. Start to make your way slowly out of this Yoga Nap by gently moving your body...

Be kind to yourself and to others as you continue throughout your day today and the rest of the week.

Happy 100th Day of Mindfulness!

You have cultivated amazing skills over the last one hundred days, and you will continue to do so in the future. Since Mindfulness is all about being present, we will celebrate Day 100 with a seated practice focusing on the present moment.

Begin in your proud seated posture. Do whatever you need to do in order to settle into this moment. Maybe it feels good to shrug your shoulders up by your ears and bring them down your back. Perhaps you drop each ear to each shoulder to stretch through your neck. Do whatever you need to do to get yourself ready for a seated practice.

Sit up tall and begin to notice your breath.
Maybe you notice it by counting your inhales and exhales.
You can pay attention to the breath moving through one of your anchors; the belly, chest, or nose.
Maybe you are using a mantra, like "I am calm", to pay attention to your breathing.
Find what feels authentic for you in this moment.

Pause for one minute.

Notice how you are feeling today - mentally, physically, and emotionally.
See if you can give yourself some space to experience whatever it is you feel.
Some days our minds are busy, some days our bodies are calm, and some days our emotions are strong. Mindful presence asks us to allow whatever we are experiencing in this moment to be okay.
While being more calm and focused is often a result of our practice, it does not always feel like that when we sit and close our eyes. It is okay if your mind is busy or focused. Remember there is no good or bad, just whatever is present. Give yourself space to experience whatever it is you are thinking and feeling today.

Pause for one minute.

Acknowledge whatever came up for you today. In the next few breaths, begin to focus on gratitude. What is something that you are grateful for right now in this moment? Can you turn all of your attention to that? Can you feel how happy it makes you to have this person or thing in your life?

Pause for a few seconds.

Think to yourself these phrases as I say them out loud
- I am calm
- I am enough
- I am grateful

Pause for a few seconds.

Now gently return your attention back to your breath. Possibly return to your counting, your anchor, or a mantra.

Pause for a few seconds.

Begin to wiggle in the fingers and toes. Keep your eyes closed and make any movements that feel good, like a stretch with your arms overhead or a twist. Turn the corners of your lips up to the sky to reveal a small smile. You have done an amazing job practicing mindfulness. You are an amazing person with unique gifts and talents. You are worthy of an amazing life and you have the ability to create it. When you are ready, open your eyes and let the world come back to you!

Resources

- Cleveland Clinic https://my.clevelandclinic.org/health/articles/11874-stress

- https://www.businessinsider.com/jim-rohn-youre-the-average-of-the-five-people-you-spend-the-most-time-with-2012-7

- https://www.youtube.com/watch?v=VTA0j8FfCvs

- https://mindfulnessexercises.com/10-inspirational-mindfulness-quotes/?utm_source=ActiveCampaign&utm_medium=email&utm_content=10+Inspirational+Mindfulness+Quotes+For+The+New+Year&utm_campaign=2019_Dec_27_10+Inspirational+Mindfulness+Quotes

- "AutoBiography in Five Chapters" by Portia Nelson

- https://www.yourtango.com/experts/chris-shea/benefits-of-meditation-mindfulness-exercises-to-use-to-be-happy-in-life

- https://www.newventureswest.com/real-lesson-taoist-farmer-story/

- https://blog.rescuetime.com/multitasking/

- https://www.considerable.com/health/mental-health/mindfulness-simple-examples/

- https://www.forbes.com/sites/jacquelynsmith/2013/09/19/quit-multitasking-how-to-unitask-and-get-more-done-2/#49393ba17d12

Music

- "Breathing Space" by Sacred Earth
- "So Long, Lonesome" by Explosions in the Sky
- "Be Here Now" by Ray LaMontange

BIOS

JULIE STRITTMATTER
(author)

Julie lives each day committed to spreading the mission of Mindfulness, beginning with herself. Practicing Mindfulness in early adulthood had such a profound impact on Julie's life that she pursued her yoga instructor certification early in her career, as well as a degree in Secondary Education. Julie believes Mindfulness is for everyone, and she is grateful to be able to share these practices with people of all ages. Julie is an E-RYT 200, Registered Children's Yoga Teacher, and holds a degree in Secondary Education English from Slippery Rock University. Julie loves finding ways to weave her passion for Mindfulness into the educational system and has been successful in doing this with her own classroom in tradition al schools, working with at-risk teens though wilderness therapy, and offering Mindfulness sessions for educators. Julie has dedicated most of her career to working with teens and was given the honor of Teacher of the Year in 2017. She is currently a content creator for Challenge to Change Inc. and owner of Sun + Soul Shine Yoga. Outside of the classroom and yoga studio, a deep love of travel, hiking, music, writing, and cooking fuels Julie's life adventures.

MOLLY SCHREIBER
(owner Challenge to Change, Inc.)

Molly Schreiber is the owner and founder of Challenge to Change, Inc, a kid's yoga studio offering lifelong wellness skills for people all of ages through the practices of fitness, yoga, meditation, and daily mindfulness practices. As a former elementary teacher, working with students and school personnel is at the heart of Molly's mission. She believes that we can change the world by empowering children with skills that foster positive thinking and compassion for self and others. This belief inspired Molly to design various programming such as The Yoga in the Schools Project, Kids and Adult Yoga Teacher Trainings, online learning resources for school and families, numerous children's books, and countless other Mindfulness resources. Molly is an E-RYT 500, Registered Children's Yoga Teacher, and holds a Master's Degree from Western Illinois University in Education. She is a mother of four beautiful children: Sydney, Maggie, Jacob, and Maria, and a wife to Tom. Regardless of the role she is in - mother, business owner, wife, friend, or teacher - Molly joyously shares her mission for helping people of all ages cultivate happy and healthy lifestyles.

MELISSA HYDE
(Editor)

Melissa Hyde is dedicated to social-emotional education in schools. A native of Los Angeles, California, Melissa received her Master of Arts in Education from Pepperdine University, then proceeded to work in a series of local schools that embraced collaborative learning, community-building, and early implementation of social-emotional standards. Melissa discovered yoga during her undergraduate years at the University of Iowa, and now works with Challenge to Change to bring yoga to children and teachers to help promote self-confidence and healthy emotional regulation skills.

Melissa brings her love of writing to Challenge to Change as their Educational Staff Writer, as well as regularly contributing to several other publications in her local area. When not practicing yoga, writing, or teaching, Melissa spends time longing for the warm weather of California and cuddling with her fur babies - Banner, a gentle standard poodle, and Skye, a very fluffy and sassy cat.

CHALLENGE TO CHANGE INC.

Challenge to Change Inc. offers signature Mindfulness programming for all ages. As a former educator, Molly Schreiber, founder and owner of Challenge to Change, keeps teachers and learners at the heart of her mission. Therefore, much of Challenge to Change's programming and resources were designed to support the happiness and health of children, teens, parents, and teachers. Located in Dubuque, Iowa, Challenge to Change spreads its mission far and wide through the use of virtual yoga classes, online training sessions, literature, and online resources.

A Classroom in Balance's 100 Mindfulness practices are featured virtually through our online platform **Peace Out Portal (POP)**. Visit challengetochangeinc.com for more information.

RESOURCES
Our easy-to-use Yoga and Mindfulness resources were developed for use in a classroom, studio, or home setting.

TRAININGS
Our 95 Hour, 200 Hour, and 300 Hour Yoga Teacher Training programs empower teachers, parents, and yogis alike to share the practices of Yoga and Mindfulness with toddlers, kids, teens, and adults.

CONTINUING EDUCATION

These courses were designed to help classroom teachers find ways to meaningfully integrate Mindfulness within their school day in a way that best serves their students and meets their scheduling needs.

PROGRAMMING

Challenge to Change's most popular program is The Yoga in the Schools Project, which provides meaningful thirty minute lessons that support the social-emotional growth of students. Our mission offers in-person lessons locally around Dubuque, IA, as well as virtual programming for our more distant learning communities.

CLASSES AND WORKSHOPS

We are always exploring new ways to share Yoga, Mindfulness, and Meditation practices with others. Join us for an in-person or virtual class or workshop. We offer sound healing, family yoga, personalized yoga classes, children's camps, yoga birthday parties, and more.

Learn more about our mission, meet the team, and explore our resources at

www.challengetochangeinc.com

Made in the USA
Las Vegas, NV
13 November 2023

80790281R00076